INTRODUCTION TO THE ART OF PLAYING ON THE PIANO FORTE

Da Capo Press Music Reprint Series

INTRODUCTION TO THE ART OF PLAYING ON THE PIANO FORTE

Containing the Elements of Music, Preliminary Notions on Fingering, and Fifty Fingered Lessons

BY MUZIO CLEMENTI

New Introduction by Sandra P. Rosenblum

DA CAPO PRESS · NEW YORK · 1974

Library of Congress Cataloging in Publication Data

Clementi, Muzio, 1752-1832.
    Introduction to the art of playing on the piano
forte.

    (Da Capo Press music reprint series)
    Reprint of the 1st ed., 2d issue, 1801, published
by Clementi, Banger, Hyde, Collard & David, London.
    "List of editions of Clementi's Introduction to the
art of playing on the piano forte and of the appendix
to the fifth edition": p.
    1. Piano—Methods. I. Title.
MT222.C617   1974   786.3'04'1   70-125067
ISBN 0-306-70004-2

Detailed bibliographic information concerning the
several editions of Muzio Clementi's *Introduction to the Art of Playing on the Piano Forte,*
first published in London in 1801, is provided
in the new introductory material prepared especially for this reprint. The second issue
of the first edition is reproduced in this volume.

INTRODUCTION

Between the years 1797 and 1804, six new keyboard methods numbering among the earliest ones written specifically for the pianoforte were published in England, Germany and France. Of these, Muzio Clementi's *Introduction to the Art of Playing on the Piano Forte* probably achieved the greatest popularity and use.[1] Originally produced in 1801, the volume was published in eleven English editions by Clementi's firm, and was also translated into French (1802), German (1802), Spanish (1809), and Italian (ca. 183?). In spite of this obvious success, most of the references to the *Introduction* in works that discuss Clementi's *oeuvre* either merely cite the volume or, at best, offer a word of praise or a comment on its commercial value to its author. The work has not been properly considered in relation to other contemporary pianoforte tutors and to the musical practice of its time.

The present reprint has been photographically reproduced from a copy of the previously unidentified second issue of the first edition, or, according to Clementi's later decision, second "edition."[2] Next to the first edition, the eighth seems to have been the most popular. It was reproduced in the United States; served as the basis of the *Méthode Complette* and *Metodo Completo* (see "List of Editions"); and its contents were probably reengraved for the unlocated ninth edition, since they were reengraved without change for the tenth, which, curiously, was assigned the opus number 42, perhaps because of the tutor's success.

This widespread use of Clementi's method might have been predicted, if only because of its author's far-reaching reputation. Many times over, during his lifetime and later, Clementi was described as the founder of the "present school" of pianoforte playing. In 1810, Fayolle wrote that he "est regardé comme le plus grande pianiste qui ait existé"[3] (a description repeated by Czerny in 1839), and Fétis, who mentioned "son excellente *Introduction*

---

[1] The other methods were, in chronological order: Johann Peter Milchmeyer's *Die Wahre Art das Pianoforte zu Spielen* (Dresden: Meinhold, 1797); Ignaz Pleyel's *Méthode pour le Pianoforte* (Paris: Pleyel, 1797); Louis Adam's *Méthode ou Principe Général du Doigté pour le Forte-Piano* (Paris: Sieber, 1798); Jan Ladislav Dussek's *Instructions on the Art of Playing the Pianoforte or Harpsichord* (London: Corri, Dussek & Co., 1799) Louis Adam's *Méthode de Piano du Conservatoire* (Paris: Au Magasin de Musique du Conservatoire Royal, 1804).

Dussek's wordy volume shows little specific relationship to the pianoforte (in contrast to the harpsichord), or to contemporary advances in technique and style of playing, except for the inclusion of relatively flexible dynamics and a cursory listing of the *una corda* pedal in the dictionary at the end. There is no discussion of touch, legato, silent finger-changing, legato octaves, and the numerous other aspects of performance that make Clementi's *Introduction* a much more significant tutor.

Pleyel's *Méthode* appears to be more comprehensive than Dussek's; but this writer was able to examine only the 3rd German edition, published in 1804 by Hoffmeister & Kühnel of Leipzig—an edition which was substantially revised by Musikdirector Schicht of Leipzig—and, therefore, finds it difficult to compare Pleyel's initial contribution to Clementi's. While Pleyel's third edition is more thorough in some areas, such as scale fingering and ornaments, it contains only one sentence about touch (indicating a general use of legato [p. 13]), and there is no mention of slurs, staccato signs, pedalling, or other indications of the "new" performance style. The few lessons are simple, uninteresting exercises.

The volumes by Milchmeyer and Adam follow the Continental predilections of the time in being far more detailed than Clementi's. Like his tutor, they contain much material that bears direct relationship to contemporary pianoforte literature and style of performance.

[2] See "List of Editions," pp. xxi–xxii. Since the second, third and fourth issues as identified by this writer, differ from the first only in partial or total reengraving but not in content, and since the publisher did not make any distinction among them, the term "first edition" will henceforth include all four issues unless a particular one is specified. A report which explains the importance and the method of identifying these issues, and includes descriptions of the successive English and Continental editions of the *Introduction* as well as of the *Appendix to the Fifth Edition of Clementi's Introduction*, is provided in a "List of Editions" at the end of this Introduction.

[3] François Fayolle & Alexandre É. Choron, *Dictionnaire Historique des Musiciens*, 2 vols. (Paris: Lenormant, 1810–11) [reprint, Hildesheim: G. Olms, 1971], I, 144.

à l'art de jouer du piano" in his *Biographie Universelle*,[4] wrote one of his many encomiums of Clementi in a "Sketch of the History of Piano-Fortes and Pianists."

> Of all the artists who have contributed to bring pianoforte playing to perfection, Clementi has been the most influential. Endowed with the most happy genius, and uniting with remarkable manual capability great method and reflection, this great artist felt the necessity of submitting the mechanism of fingering, and the art of drawing the tone from the instrument, to certain fixed and invariable rules. Without prejudice to his brilliant imagination, these two important parts of his art became the object of his studies, and the result was, the most perfect organization of the articulation of the fingers possible to imagine. The school of Clementi is considered by the most able pianists as the best among the many that have been founded.[5]

Clementi's new technical and stylistic concepts are developed to their full extent in his finer sonatas and in the *Gradus ad Parnassum*. This tutor was designed primarily as a succinct introduction to the basic knowledge required by the rapidly-growing class of amateur music-makers. Nevertheless, the brief remarks and exercises were sufficient to reveal to the observant reader and skillful teacher of the time the germ of the new technical skills and interpretative knowledge needed for performance of the emerging piano literature. Thus, this volume, which was more up-to-date than many others written between 1800 and 1820, discloses significant details concerning the transitional state of keyboard performance at the turn of the century, some twenty years after the pianoforte achieved primacy among the keyboard instruments.

*   *   *   *   *

Born in Rome in 1752, only two years after the death of J.S. Bach, Clementi was taken to England in 1766 by Peter Beckford, who offered to serve as the boy's patron.[6] Until 1773 Clementi lived at Stepleton House in Dorset County, one hundred miles from London. There, in the extensive library of his wealthy patron, he found the books from which he acquired his vast knowledge of languages and literature, and the works of many composers of different styles including Corelli, Handel, A. Scarlatti, J.S. Bach, J.C. Bach, and Paradies. Having passed the organist's exam in Italy at the age of nine, and having studied advanced counterpoint there under Carpani, the young man was already a skilled musician when Beckford discovered him. There is no record of his having had any teachers during his residence at Stepleton.

According to Clementi's conversation with the pianist Amédée Méreaux in 1820, his daily routine of study while residing with the Beckfords included eight hours of practice on the harpsichord.[7] Although England was the earliest country to espouse the new pianoforte,[8] no proof is provided in any reliable report for the presence of such an instrument at Stepleton while Clementi lived there,[9] nor has any information become available from inventories of

---

[4] François Joseph Fétis, *Biographie Universelle des Musiciens*, 10 vols. (Bruxelles: Meline, Cans et Compagnie, 1837) [reprint Brussels: Editions Culture et Civilisation, 1972], III, 161–2.

[5] *Harmonicon* (Sept. 1831), 213. This article had originally appeared in *La Révue Musicale*.

[6] Peter Beckford was a cousin of William Beckford, author of *Vathek*, who resided at Fonthill Abbey, Wiltshire.

[7] Amédée Méreaux, *Les Clavecinistes de 1637 à 1790* (Paris: Heugel & Cie., 1867) 75.

[8] Its first public exposure was provided by Dibdin, who accompanied songs on a piano at a benefit concert for Miss Brickler in May 1767. In 1768 J.C. Bach played a Zumpe square piano as a solo instrument at a public concert. (Rosamond Harding, *The Pianoforte: Its History Traced to the Great Exhibition of 1851* [Cambridge: Cambridge University Press, 1933] 67.)

[9] In her unpublished manuscript, *Muzio Clementi and His Era* (a property of the Yale University Music Library, p. 45), Renze Wilshire, a great grand-daughter of the composer, stated that a new Broadwood piano was purchased for Clementi's use at Stepleton. However, this romanticized biography lacks any documentation for this (as well as other statements), and such a piano could not have been a Broadwood, since that firm did not begin to make pianos until 1773, the year in which Clementi moved to London.

Peter Beckford's estate or other legal documents. It is possible that Clementi's first opportunity for continued contact with the new instrument occurred only after he moved to the city.[10] In 1773, widely read and equipped with a thorough command of the keyboard, he went to London, where, with the exception of concert tours and a few extended sojourns on the Continent,[11] he lived most of the remaining 60 years of his life.

Clementi's present reputation unjustifiably rests largely on his sonatinas and on some poor editions of his *Gradus ad Parnassum*, from which the more interesting pieces had been omitted; yet his sonatas enjoyed an enviable reputation on the Continent, in England, and in America during his lifetime and into the mid-nineteenth century. Many eminent teachers, among them Kalkbrenner, Czerny, Dionysus Weber (first director of The Prague Conservatory), and Chopin, taught and recommended his sonatas as well as his studies.[12] Certainly, several of his more inspired works deserve a prominent position in the mainstream of piano literature.

Clementi was one of the earliest composers to conceive keyboard compositions completely in terms of the pianoforte, and the first to exploit many facets of the new instrument. The Sonatas of Opus 2, published in 1779[13] — the same year in which Clementi initially played the piano in public—burst upon the unsuspecting musical world demanding flamboyant double-note passages, especially thirds and sixths, and rapid octaves, and greatly extending the contemporary concepts of keyboard technique. Composers, performers, and teachers had to reckon with this new technical material as well as with the style of his more "serious" works of the 1780's, all of which had a significant influence on the writing for piano of men as diverse as Beethoven, Louis Adam,[14] and the Portuguese João Domingo Bomtempo.[15] The best of the subsequent tutors, such as those by Adam and Milchmeyer (see footnote 1), also reflected the changes in scope of technique with the inclusion of new challenges in their exercises.

Beethoven admired and, according to Schindler,[16] owned most of the sonatas by Clementi.

---

[10] Apparently Clementi did not appear in public as a pianist until a concert in London on April 23, 1779, almost 6 years after he had moved there. He had played the harpsichord for his few concert appearances in 1775, 1778 and earlier in 1779. (Max Unger, *Muzio Clementis Leben* [Langensalza: Herman Beyer & Söhne, 1914] 16.)

[11] The chief biographic work remains Max Unger's *Muzio Clementis Leben* (Langensalza: Herman Beyer & Söhne, 1914) [reprint, New York: Da Capo Press, 1971], from which Georges de Saint-Foix drew the details of Clementi's life for his article, "Muzio Clementi (1752–1832)," *The Musical Quarterly* IX 3 (July 1923), 350–82. Brief biographies are found in *Musik in Geschichte und Gegenwart*, Friedrich Blume, ed. (Kassel: Bärenreiter, 1952); *Grove's Dictionary of Music and Musicians*, 5th edition, Eric Blom, ed. (New York: St. Martin's Press, 1954); and *Enciclopedia della Musica*, Claudio Sartori, ed. (Milan: G. Ricordi, 1963). In the latter two, only the French edition of the *Introduction* is cited.

An interesting anonymous account of Clementi's life appeared in the *Quarterly Musical Magazine and Review* II (1820). Tyson [for full reference, see following paragraph] p. 12) believes this article to have been written by W.F. Collard, Clementi's business partner and friend, with information probably dervied from Clementi. It reappeared in Sainsbury's *Dictionary of Musicians* (1824) [reprint, New York: Da Capo Press, 1966]; again, with additions, in *Apollo's Gift, or the Musical Souvenir for MDCCCXXXI*; and formed the basis of the "Memoir of Muzio Clementi" in the *Harmonicon* (August 1831). These accounts, in turn, served as the basis for many of the later dictionary sketches. Not surprisingly, the *Introduction* is mentioned in a most favorable light.

Alan Tyson's important *Thematic Catalogue of the Works of Muzio Clementi* (Tutzing: Hans Schneider, 1967) provides some bibliographic information on various editions of the *Introduction*. Other pertinent studies include Giulio Cesare Paribeni, *Muzio Clementi nella vita e nell'arte* (Milan: Podrecca, 1921); Riccard Allorto, *Le Sonate per pianoforte di Muzio Clementi, studio critico e cataloga tematica* (Florence: Olschki, 1959); Elena di Laura, *L'Estetica nell'arte didattica di Muzio Clementi* (Rome: Tipografia Armani, 1934); Carl G. Parrish, "The Early Piano and Its Influence on Keyboard Technique and Composition in the Eighteenth Century" (Unpublished Ph.D. dissertation, Harvard University, 1939); and Bianca Becherini, "Il 'Metodo' per Pianoforte di Muzio Clementi," *Rivista Musicale Italiana* XLIII, (1939), 55–71. This last essay is a somewhat flowery discussion of the *Metodo Completo* (see "List of Editions," III, E, page xxxix).

In several of these accounts the country estate of Peter Beckford has mistakenly been called Fonthill Abbey, which was the home of his cousin William Beckford of questionable repute. Unger, St. Foix, Paribeni, Allorto, Riemann (*Musiklexikon*), Hans Engel (*Musik in Geschichte und Gegenwart*), and di Laura are among those who have perpetuated this confusion. (See footnote 6.)

[12] In the Appendix to his *Kunst des Vortrags* (1842), Czerny published a list, with incipits, of the "best and most useful works of all known composers for the pianoforte, from Mozart to the present time." After an extensive list of works by Mozart, including five concerti, he suggestes only two sonatas by Haydn (both of the great ones in E-flat major), but then thirteen sonatas by Clementi, spanning his *oeuvre* from Opus 2/2 to Opus 40/3, and also the *Gradus ad Parnassum*.

[13] Tyson, *Clementi Catalogue*, 36. The date 1773, given in earlier books on Clementi, is without substantiation.

[14] William S. Newman, *The Sonata in the Classic Era* (Chapel Hill: The University of North Carolina Press, 1963), 657.

[15] William S. Newman, *The Sonata since Beethoven* (Chapel Hill: The University of North Carolina Press, 1969), 655.

[16] Anton Schindler, *The Life of Beethoven*, Ignaz Moscheles, ed. (London: 1841) [republished, Boston: Oliver Ditson, ca. 1841], 135n.

At Beethoven's request, Carl Czerny taught Beethoven's nephew, Karl, these sonatas for some time. Beethoven's interest in Clementi's works no doubt accounts in part for his having the *Introduction* used as Karl's tutor, even though more thorough ones were available.[17] Unger, however, claims that Beethoven chose the volume because of its conciseness and intelligibility.[18] In 1826 Beethoven sent Mollo's German edition of the *Introduction* to his lifelong friend, Stephan von Breuning, for the instruction of his thirteen-year old son, Gerhard. The book was accompanied by a note saying: "If he uses it as I will show him, it will certainly produce good results."[19] The choice of this tutor was an expressed preference over both "Czerny's *Klavierschule*"[20] and Pleyel's *Méthode*, which Gerhard already had.

In addition to his acclaim as a virtuoso pianist—perhaps the first—and as a composer, Clementi was reputed to be an urbane man of broad cultural interests, and was admired for his success in an unusual variety of other musical endeavors. Sought-after teacher, orchestral conductor, knowledgeable publisher, successful piano manufacturer, astute businessman—he ranks among the most versatile of musicians. He was also extremely influential. Through his compositions, concerts, teaching, didactic works,[21] and improvements in piano tone and structure,[22] Clementi left an indelible mark on the style of composition and performance for the developing instrument.

*   *   *   *   *

[17] In 1816, when Czerny began teaching Karl, the choice would have included the methods by Milchmeyer and A.E. Müller as well as German translations of those by Pleyel and Adam.

[18] Unger, op. cit., 112.

[19] Gerhard von Breuning, *Aus dem Schwarzspanierhause* (Wien: Verlag von L. Rosner, 1874), 70–71. Beethoven's letter to Haslinger requested "Clementi's *Clavierschule* translated into German." The edition procured, of several available, was Mollo's, first published about 1806.

[20] Emily Anderson, ed., *Letters of Beethoven*, 3 vols. (New York: St. Martin's Press, 1961), III, 1279. Since it has not been possible to trace a *Klavierschule* by Carl Czerny published prior to the date of this letter (Spring 1826), Beethoven may have been referring to *Der Wiener Klavierlehrer* by Joseph Czerny, with whom Beethoven was also acquainted. This tutor was published by Haslinger in 1825.

[21] Clementi's first purely didactic work was the *Introduction*. It was followed in November 1801 and February 1802 by the first and second volumes of his *Selection of Practical Harmony for the Organ or Pianoforte*, which is numbered by Tyson WO 7 ("without opus-number") [op. cit., 103]. From 1802 to 1810 Clementi travelled on the Continent. The third volume of the *Practical Harmony* was published on his return (announced in the *Morning Post* on February 18, 1811, [Tyson, op. cit., 103], the same day as the fifth edition of the *Introduction*), followed by the *Appendix to the Fifth Edition of the Introduction*, Opus 43, also in 1811. The concluding volume of *Practical Harmony* appeared in 1815, and the three volumes of *Gradus ad Parnassum*, Opus 44, in 1817, 1819 and 1826. The *Gradus*, Clementi's final exposition of pianoforte technique, contains everything of significance demanded of the pianist until the advent of Chopin's *Etudes*, yet maintains a balance between technical and artistic values. The one hundred pieces are for advanced students, and volumes two and three each present problems more difficult than those in the preceding volumes.

The pieces included in *Preludes and Exercises*, which both Paribeni and Allorto list as having been published in 1790, seem, in fact, to have been published initially as part of the *Appendix to the Fifth Edition* (see page xxxii). They were later extracted and published as a separate volume by André, Mollo, Peters, and other firms. No evidence is available to support the earlier publication date.

[22] Although various writers have alluded to improvements on the construction of the piano made by Clementi himself, these have never been documented, and there are no patents in his name. In the official record of *Patents for Inventions* published by the British Office of the Commissioner of Patents, there are two patents in the name of William Frederick Collard, one of Clementi's partners. The patent of 1811 makes changes on the hitch pinblock, the wrest pin block, and in the placing of the hammers and dampers on upright pianos, thus improving the tone and making it easier to string the instruments. The patent of 1821 includes the addition of a "bridge of reverberation" to aid the "vibration of the strings and enrich the sound." (see *Patents for Inventions* [London: 1871], 67–8, 87–8.) Whether the origin of these inventions stemmed from Clementi himself will probably never be known; however they were discussed in both English and foreign music journals. According to Unger (op. cit., 248), Clementi reported further improvements to Härtel in Leipzig in July 1826. These concerned resistance to heat and cold and a new method of stringing instruments.

Letters written to Collard from the Continent between 1803 and 1808 indicate that Clementi was seriously concerned about the variation in action and tone among the pianos that Collard was shipping to Europe to fill orders arranged by his travelling partner. Clementi went so far as to suggest the possibility that perhaps "our manufacture" has "considerably *suffered by my absence*." He also purchased strings in Europe for their pianos. On August 31, 1805 he wrote Collard: "Since you find the strings good, send for more immediately, for the tone of instruments depends *much* on that article; and stinginess in such cases is the highest folly" (unpublished letter in the Wilshire *Nachlass*, property of the Yale University Music Library).

Clementi pianos were popular among those imported into the United States. They were advertised by G. Graupner, 6 Franklin Street, Boston, as "Clementi's new patent Pianofortes superior to any others yet known," (title page, Gottlieb Graupner, *Rudiments of the Art of playing on the Piano Forte* [Boston: G. Graupner, 1806]) and many are still extant in New England and the New York area.

Clementi's *Introduction* is a slim volume, and, viewed as a whole, better suited to the needs of large numbers of relatively inexperienced students and amateurs than to the instruction of advanced performers. In this respect it was typical of all the English and of some of the French methods of the late eighteenth and early nineteenth centuries, whose authors provided only brief discussions of fingering, technique, ornaments, and other matters. Judging by contemporary criticism, conciseness was a prerequisite of a successful English tutor, for these books of instruction "devoted to the education of young musicians" were considered in their time

> as dictionaries of elements, rather than as a positive determinate series of lessons, to be applied indiscriminately in the order and succession in which they are printed . . . After all then, these are merely the chest of tools—it is the master who must direct the employment of them.[23]

No doubt Clementi was also guided at this time (around 1800), the initial period of his publishing activities, by business as well as pedagogic considerations.

Clementi's *Introduction* was criticized in Germany for its lack of detail, but the Germans had a different approach to the writing of tutors, most of which were voluminous, and occasionally given to considerable verbosity. Some contained a few short musical compositions; others, none. On the other hand, the *Introduction* had an unmistakeable influence on several French, English, and American methods. These include Adam's *Méthode* of 1804, J. B. Cramer's *Instructions for the Pianoforte,* a tutor by Neville Butler Challoner published both in London and Philadelphia, and one by Gottlieb Graupner, published in Boston, in which many pages of text, including the important sections on style and ornaments, and one-third of the lessons, are taken verbatim from Clementi's *Introduction.*[24]

Clementi followed the basic arrangement used by most late-eighteenth-century English instruction books — a short section describing the elements of music, sometimes followed by fingered scales and/or a few exercises, and lastly, a small number of pieces or lessons. Although still brief, Clementi's descriptions of the materials of music, signs of notation and expression, and ornaments are more extensive and far more interesting than those of his predecessors, including Hook, Broderip, and Dussek.[25] He also included fingered scales and a very important group of exercises, as well as a prelude in each key to introduce the lessons.

The most significant aspect of Clementi's mature playing, in addition to his new technical developments, was his expressive legato style, which is an indispensable ingredient for the performance of the slow movements of his sonatas. The importance he attached to the overall use of legato is made clear in the *Introduction* (pages 8–9, 15, 17). The English piano of his time, from which the modern grand piano evolved, had a heavier touch (caused by a deeper key dip) and thicker strings than those made in Vienna, and, therefore, a much more sonorous tone. This allowed Clementi to develop a broad, expressive style of performance, dependent, in large measure, on legato technique.

During much of the eighteenth century the basic keyboard touch (exclusive of organ playing) had been non-legato, as described by Türk in 1789:

---

[23] Comments by an anonymous reviewer of a group of new piano methods in the *Quarterly Musical Magazine and Review* (1820), 99-104. The methods of Clementi and Cramer are also cited in addition to those being reviewed.

[24] Johann Baptist Cramer, *Instructions for the Pianoforte* (London: Chappell, [1812]); Neville Butler Challoner, *A New Preceptor for the Piano Forte,* from the Second London Edition, ca. 1810 (Philadelphia: G. E. Blake, n.d.); Gottlieb Graupner, op. cit.

Graupner, who asserted a strong musical influence in Boston between 1797 and 1836, had lived in London from 1788 to about 1796. While he was primarily an oboist and one of the founders in Boston of both the Handel and Haydn Society and the Philharmonic Society, he was also well-known as a piano teacher, and must have had sent to him, or purchased in America, a copy of Clementi's tutor.

[25] James Hook, *Guida di Musica,* Op. 37 (London: Preston, ca. 1785); Robert Broderip, *A Short Introduction to the Art of Playing the Harpsichord,* Op. 6 (London: Longman and Broderip, 179?).

When notes are to be played in the usual way, that is, neither staccato nor
legato, the finger should be raised from the key a little earlier than the value
of the note requires.[26]

The slur was used to indicate legato playing, which was cultivated to a considerably greater
degree in slow movements than in fast ones.

The first tutor to advocate legato as the basic keyboard touch is a surprisingly early,
rather obscure work, *The Art of Fingering the Harpsichord*, by Nicolo Pasquali, an Italian
living in Edinburgh. In this interesting volume Pasquali writes:

The Legato is the Touch that this Treatise endeavours to teach, being a general
Touch fit for almost all Kinds of Passages, and by which the Vibrations of
the Strings are made perfect in every Note.[27]

With the increasing use of the piano after 1780, there was a gradual change toward more
use of legato touch; nevertheless it was several decades before exaggerated reactions to
"choppy playing" no longer gained attention.[28]

Although he did not attempt the kind of detailed description of touch written by Milchmeyer,[29]
it was Clementi who, by the combination of his concertizing and teaching, and the widespread
use of his tutor, popularized the expressive legato style, which became the preferred keyboard
touch of the nineteenth century. In the *Introduction* his remarks on "style" begin with the
statement, "The best general rule, is to keep down the keys of the instrument, the FULL
LENGTH of every note; . . ." unless they are marked otherwise (page 8). After contrasting
that with three kinds of staccato, he describes briefly the manner of playing legato "by
which means, the strings VIBRATE SWEETLY into one another" (page 9). He did not
specifically mention the kind of overlapping of notes described for particular usages by
Milchmeyer, but that manner of playing may well have been intended where necessary to
attain the desired legato or legatissimo. In conclusion Clementi adds:

---

[26] Daniel Gottlob Türk, *Klavierschule* (Leipzig: Schwickert, 1789) [reprint, Kassel: Bärenreiter, 1962]; 356.

[27] Nicolo Pasquali, *The Art of Fingering the Harpischord* (Edinburgh: Bremner, ca. 1760), 26.

[28] In a letter to Streicher, the piano manufacturer, in 1796, Beethoven made the following interesting comment:
There is no doubt that so far as the manner of playing it is concerned, the *pianoforte* is still
the least studied and developed of all instruments; often one thinks that one is merely listening
to a harp. And I am delighted, my dear fellow, that you are one of the few who realize and
perceive that, provided one can feel the music, one can also make the pianoforte sing. I hope
that the time will come when the harp and the pianoforte will be treated as two entirely different
instruments. [Emily Anderson, ed., *Letters of Beethoven*, I, 25–6.]
From about 1792, when Beethoven became widely acclaimed in Vienna as a virtuoso pianist, to the early 1800's, when composition
began to occupy most of his time and oncoming deafness must have interfered with his playing, he cultivated and developed the legato
to an extent considered remarkable at that time. Without citing any evidence, two writers have attributed this to the influence of Clementi.
Since Beethoven's interest in legato touch antedates any of the well-known, turn-of-the-century tutors that advocated its general use,
and since Beethoven had not heard Clementi play, it would seem more likely that the root lay either in some other influence, or just
in the process of adapting to what sounded best on the new keyboard instrument. It may be significant that both Clementi and Beethoven
had been accomplished organists in their early years, for which they would have cultivated a fine legato touch. Di Laura states that
when Clementi was asked, during his stay in Vienna, about his ideal for pianists, he replied that it was "to imitate with the sound
of the piano, the legato style and grandness of the organ and the orchestra" (op. cit., 17).

[29] Milchmeyer was the first, in 1797, to attempt to describe in detail the use of touch appropriate to the pianoforte. His *usual* way
of playing was legato, lifting the finger from one key when the next was played. However he also described a "slurred" way of playing
which required that "the fingers remain somewhat longer, and on several notes" (op. cit., 6). This overlapping of notes was restricted
to particular types of passages in the different ranges of the keyboard. Milchmeyer's specifications for touch produce excellent results
on the Broadwood piano built in 1804, with a range of five and one-half octaves from FFF to c''', that is in the instrument collection
of the Museum of Fine Arts in Boston. For example, in the upper octave and a half of that instrument the overlapping of notes is
essential to a satisfactory legato sound, just as Milchmeyer suggested; from c' down to the bass the "usual way of playing" results
in a fine legato.

> N. B. When the composer leaves the LEGATO, and STACCATO to the per-
> former's taste; the best rule is, to adhere chiefly to the LEGATO; reserving
> the STACCATO to give SPIRIT occasionally to certain passages, and to set
> off the HIGHER BEAUTIES of the LEGATO.

A more direct statement of the place of legato touch on the new keyboard instrument
can hardly be imagined. This precept is further reinforced by the reminder, preceding the
first simple exercise on page 15, "to keep down the first key 'till the second has been
struck, and so on," and by emphasis on silent finger changing (page 17) and legato octaves
(page 19). It is interesting to note, however, that while his mature playing was acclaimed
for its singing legato style, Clementi had not always played that way. In a widely-reported
conversation between Clementi and his student Ludwig Berger, in 1806, Berger asked Clementi
whether he had treated the instrument in his present style at the time of the famous competition
with Mozart arranged by Emperor Joseph II in 1781. Clementi

> answered in the negative, adding that in those early days he still preferred
> to display his talents by brilliant execution, especially in double-note passages
> which were not customary prior to him, and in improvisations; only later had
> he adapted the more cantabile and refined style of performance by listening
> attentively to singers celebrated at the time, and also through the gradual
> perfection particularly of the English pianos, whose earlier faulty construction
> virtually precluded a cantabile, legato style of playing.[30]

Field, Cramer, Kalkbrenner, and other students of Clementi were among the most popular
pianists of their day.[31] They were all admired for their exquisite cantabile legato style,
and were influential in establishing its importance in nineteenth-century piano playing. Field
and Berger reflected and passed on the influence of their teacher also through their lyric
piano pieces.

Louis Adam, an important professor at the Paris Conservatoire, describes pianoforte touch
in some detail in his *Méthode* of 1804. Unfortunately, his writing is not always well organized
and is sometimes ambiguous. In this tutor, which was adopted by the Conservatoire and saw
five editions in Paris as well as a bilingual French-German edition, he paraphrased, and
hence publicized, Clementi's final statement about touch as follows:

> Sometimes the composer indicates the musical phrase that ought to be slurred,
> but when he leaves the choice of *legato* or *staccato* to the taste of the performer,
> the latter should adhere chiefly to the *legato*, reserving the *staccato* to emphasize
> certain passages and, by an artful contrast, to evoke the advantages of the
> *legato*.[32]

*   *   *   *   *

---

[30] Ludwig Berger, "Erläuterung eines Mozart' schen Urtheils über Muzio Clementi," *Allgemeine Musikalische Zeitung* XXXI/27 (July
1829), col. 468.

  Mozart's well-known disparaging remarks, written in letters to his family, that Clementi was a mere "mechanicus" who excelled in
showing off double thirds and sixths but who played without "a farthing's worth of taste or feeling," stem from this encounter. (Emily
Anderson, ed., *Letters of Mozart*, 2 vols. [London: Macmillan, 1966], II, 793.) Mozart may have felt discomfort in the face of a stronger
technician and of changing keyboard styles; yet the comments were probably justified to an extent, as Clementi's own report to Berger
seems to indicate.

[31] A roster of the famous students of Clementi includes, in addition to the three mentioned, Madame Gaetano Bartholozzi (the former
Therese Jansen), Ludwig Berger, Benoît Auguste Bertini, Johann N. Hummel, Alexander Klengel, Charles Mayer, Giacomo Meyerbeer,
Ignaz Moscheles, and Karl Traugott Zeuner. Berger and Field were teachers of great repute, and it is evident from reports of their
students' playing that they passed on Clementi's style.

[32] Adam, *Méthode de Piano*, 151.

Clementi's examples of ornaments include only appoggiaturas, turns, trills, and mordents, and, on page 9, the somewhat old-fashioned arpeggio with acciaccatura. This is a much smaller number than that discussed by Carl Philipp Emanuel Bach[33] or Türk, who are far more comprehensive in their coverage of the subject. Clementi's treatment reflects the reduction in both type and number of ornaments used at the end of the century, as well as his penchant for brevity. For the most part, his realizations of ornaments are firmly rooted in eighteenth-century traditions, but in his realizations of trills there are some significant gestures towards the future.

During the second half of the eighteenth century, it was common practice for the short trill in a line of rapid descending seconds to begin on the main note rather than the upper auxiliary. Clementi, however, was among the earlier authors to show *only* a three-note realization for all uses of the short trill (page 11). Many contemporary and later tutors, including those of Dussek (1799) and Cramer (1812), continued to suggest only the older, upper-auxiliary start, or a choice of realization.[34]

Clementi's example of a trill approached from below in a stepwise legato line (page 11) is also of some significance. While trills slurred to their upper-auxiliary note in a descending line had been realized in many eighteenth-century tutors either with the upper auxiliary *or* the main note falling on the beat, there had been almost no discussion of trills in ascending stepwise legato lines. Lacassagne, in his treatise on singing, showed a series of trills in a rising line and suggested starting them on the main note.[35] Clementi's seems to have been the first keyboard tutor in which such a single trill was realized, and it is shown commencing on the main note, thus giving precedence to the melodic line—a point of view more widely embraced later, in the nineteenth century—rather than to the harmonic dissonance often achieved with an upper-auxiliary start. Adam adopted Clementi's realization in his *Méthode* of 1804.

The sole realization of appoggiaturas which is different from that shown in other late eighteenth-century tutors, is 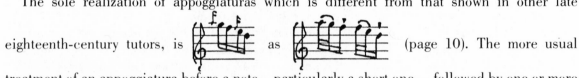 as (page 10). The more usual treatment of an appoggiatura before a note—particularly a short one— followed by one or more notes of the same value, forming a rhythmic group, would have been as an invariable short appoggiatura, with more length given to the first main note than to the ornament. Clementi's realization is all the more surprising since, in most editions after the first, "In quick time" is indicated under the four sixteenths. The only other sources of the period in which this realization is found are Adam's *Méthode* of 1804 (although not his *Méthode* published in 1798), and the tutors of Challoner and Graupner, all mentioned earlier as having been strongly influenced by Clementi's *Introduction*.

One aspect of the performance of turns that is alluded to indirectly in Galeazzi's *Elementi di Musica*, Part I, of 1791, is stated clearly by Clementi: "N.B. The Lowest note of EVERY sort of turn is MOSTLY a semitone" (page 11). Very few theorists describe the intervallic structure of turns, although the number of exceptions to Clementi's statement in the tutors of nearly two centuries is negligible. The three turns on pages 10 and 11 whose lowest notes are a whole step below the main note, have only a half step between the uppermost and main notes. The real meaning, then, for performers is that the interval embraced by

---

[33] Carl Philipp Emanuel Bach, *Versuch über die wahre Art das Clavier zu spielen*, 1753; Eng. trans. William J. Mitchell (New York: W.W. Norton, 1949).

[34] In the eighth and later editions the transient shake was realized as a triplet, rather than with the first two notes faster than the third. In rapid tempi, this is certainly easier to play with short note values.

[35] Abbé Joseph Lacassagne, *Traité général des éléments du chant* (Paris: Printed for the author, 1766), 48.

a turn should generally be a minor third; most often the minor second is between the two lower notes, although it may also be between the upper ones.

Occasionally Clementi's awareness of change in musical style is shown by a specific comment. After demonstrating all types of "beats" or mordents, long, short, prepared and unprepared, that had been used in earlier music, he concludes: "Lastly, let us remark, that the beat is seldom used in modern music" (page 12). Clementi was not alone in his views. Adam omitted the mordent in the *Méthode* of 1804, and, in his *Neue Singe-Schule* of the same year, J. F. Schubert states, "This ornament no longer suits today's taste . . . "[36] Clementi curtailed his discussion of the beat in the eighth edition (ca. 1814–16), where, after the same five realizations shown in the first edition, he writes:

> The LENGTH of the BEAT is determined by the circumstances of the passage; and the undernote is mostly a semitone. In modern music, however, we make no use of the long or continued Beat, but the short Beat ♪♪♪ has, sometimes, a good effect for the sake of emphasis.

From Hummel's *Clavierschule* (1828) onward, the mordent was universally omitted from all tutors not historically oriented.

Another comment of particular interest to performers is: "N.B. The second part of a piece, if VERY LONG, is seldom repeated; notwithstanding the DOTS" (page 8). This would certainly apply to some of Clementi's own works, including the third movement of the important and beautiful *Sonata in F minor*, variously numbered Op. 13, No. 6, or Op. 14, No. 3,[37] as well as to some works by his contemporaries.

Clementi continued to use *rinforzando* (page 9) in its earlier meaning—to indicate a short crescendo — rather than turning to the usage that became popular in some quarters just a few years later — to emphasize a single note or chord. Yet he seems to have been the first to introduce an imperceptible slackening of the tempo into the definition of *calando*. This term was used in the nineteenth century just as it is described on page 14, although previously it had only been a synonym for decrescendo. The definition of *con espressione* or *con anima*, on page 14, is a clear indication of the depth of feeling with which Clementi must have played some of his sonata movements. Finally it should be noted, because of its frequent appearance in his music, that contrary to most French and German composers, Clementi (and his pupil Cramer) followed an Italian custom of designating the slowest tempo *Adagio*, rather than *Largo* or *Grave*.

*　*　*　*　*

The piano in common use around 1801 had a range of five octaves, FF-f''', and the exercises and pieces in the first edition of the *Introduction* fall within these limits. Starting in 1794, however, a few pianos were made with "additional" keys; and in that same year Clementi composed his *Sonata*, Op. 33, No. 1, "for Instruments, with or without additional Keys." The notes from f-sharp''' to c'''', requiring a keyboard of five and a half octaves, appear in three lessons in the fifth edition (1811) of the tutor (and are used in all subsequent editions), but it was not until the seventh edition (ca. 1812–14) that they were added to the description of the keyboard on page 1 and the exercises on page 2.

Although several types of pedals were common on pianos of both English and Continental manufacture when this volume was written, and were discussed in some detail by both Milchmeyer and Adam, there is no mention of them in the original *Introduction*. Clementi

---

[36] Johann Friedrich Schubert, *Neue Singe-Schule* (Leipzig: Breitkopf & Härtel, 1804), 67.

[37] Clementi's revised and greatly improved version of this *Sonata in F minor*, the manuscript of which is in the Library of Congress, has been published by E.C. Schirmer Music Co. of Boston in an edition prepared by this writer. Interestingly, while the second part of the third movement has a repeat sign at the beginning, there is none at the end, and the autograph is marked *Fine*.

may have dismissed the harp pedal and other similar devices (holdovers from the harpsichord built into some pianos) as insignificant for the developing new instrument. Most English upright and grand pianos of Clementi's time, however, were equipped with both damper and *una corda* pedals;[38] but it was not until the fifth edition that the following brief remark was added, rather hastily, judging by the uneven spacing of the typography, to the list of expression marks on page 9: "Ped: signifies to put down the pedal, which raises the dampers; and this mark ✪ to let it go again." The only lesson in this edition for which use of the pedal is indicated is a *Spanish Air* arranged by Steibelt. The *una corda* pedal is not mentioned.

This scanty treatment of such an important aspect of piano playing is curious. The conservative Hummel, overreacting to the tendency among pianists to abuse the new device, wrote: "Neither Mozart, nor Clementi, required these means to earn the highly-deserved reputation of being the greatest, and most expressive keyboard performers of their day."[39] Yet, it seems certain that Clementi used the damper pedal in his playing. There are only a few scattered indications for its use in the sonatas, but many in the *Gradus ad Parnassum*. Its omission in the first edition of the *Introduction,* and its brief treatment thereafter, can probably be laid partly to the view that this volume was intended for relatively inexperienced students for whom use of the damper pedal would have been of negligible importance and, possibly, too difficult. None of the lessons in the first edition needed it, and its use could have been introduced when the teacher chose. Since all the British tutors of this period were intended for about the same level of pianist, and since, traditionally, they were brief, none discussed the subject of pedalling.

From the seventh edition on, and in the *Appendix,* occasional use of the damper pedal is indicated in the preludes and lessons. Having played this material on one of Clementi's pianos, the writer was led to conclude that there are passages in which either the composer forgot to insert signs to raise or change the pedal, or the engraver omitted them or inadvertently shifted them a beat or so to the right. Similar instances arise in some of Clementi's sonatas, both in autograph and printed sources. Some pedal indications that may appear questionable to pianists more accustomed to the sonority of the modern grand piano, however, sound completely appropriate on the early nineteenth-century instrument with its thinner, shorter-lived tone.

Clementi was probably the first writer to make the point that the easiest fingering may not also be the best for achieving the desired musical effect (page 14). While not discussed fully, fingering is demonstrated in the scales, exercises, and lessons. Clementi notated fingering according to the prevailing English custom, using + for the thumb. This was altered to 1 in the Continental editions.

The style of fingering is generally modern in concept, most of the restrictions of the earlier eighteenth century having been abandoned as the increased interest in legato playing demanded more flexibility and greater use of the thumb. The scale fingering is the same as that used today, with the exceptions of the right-hand fingering for F-sharp minor and C-sharp minor. In the melodic form, these scales are usually played with a change of fingers as the descent begins, allowing for the easiest fingering: the thumb is placed immediately before black notes when the scale descends, as it is used immediately following them in the ascending form. This gives the descending form of the melodic minor scale the same fingering as its relative major—an arrangement that had been shown as early as 1753 by C.P.E. Bach and later by Pleyel (3rd ed., 1804) and Adam (1804). In 1789 Türk presented both the old and this new fingering, leaving the choice to the performer. In the first edition

---

[38] Square pianos often had another type of mute pedal, such as the lute, instead of the *una corda,* which was not mechanically compatible with their construction.

[39] Johann Nepomuk Hummel, *Ausführliche Theoretisch-practische Anweisung zum Piano-Forte Spiel* (Vienna: Haslinger, 1828), III, 437.

of the *Introduction,* Clementi specified the older fingering, with the same pattern of fingers used up and down the scale. This was also used by Müller in 1804, and, curiously, by Rafael Joseffy early in the twentieth century. However, by the time of the fifth edition, Clementi had adopted the more modern fingering (see page xxiii, "List of Editions").

Clementi's avoidance of the thumb on black notes (except in chords that required it) was a conservative practice. This stricture had been adhered to by his predecessors, but was gradually abandoned later for practical reasons. On the other hand, his attitude that finger changing on repeated notes was necessary only when the notes repeated quickly or when there were other specific reasons, was more realistic than that of most later nineteenth-century editors, who prescribed it automatically and indiscriminately.

Clementi writes that "all unnecessary motion [of the hand and arm] must be avoided" (page 15). For the importance he placed on this precept in his teaching, as well as for his way of implementing it, we have evidence from his pupil John Field, who used to practice with coins on the backs of his hands.

In keeping with the new technical demands for performance, Clementi's section of fingered exercises places considerable emphasis on the playing of thirds and sixths, legato octaves, and silent finger-changing. Most of the exercises are brief; some are only initial formulae meant to be expanded, and they were probably all meant to be transposed. The skillful teacher could also create additional exercises based on these models.

Another interesting innovation is the use of the arpeggiated diminished-seventh chord. This has since played an important role in many "schools" of technique that stress independence and equality of the fingers, including that of Isidor Philipp, who based almost all his exercises on it. Clementi's concern for these two aspects of technique is made clear by his comments and exercises in the *Gradus*—a work in which he extends to new heights all the functions of technique observed in the *Introduction,* including equality, agility, double notes, repeated notes, and trills.

In the eighth edition of the *Introduction,* Clementi added exercises to facilitate sliding from a black to a white key with one finger—a device often helpful in legato playing. And to make more emphatic the importance of equality of the hands, he wrote out more exercises for the left hand, showing how to invert the ones notated only for the right hand. While introducing most of the demands required by the new advances in piano playing, the exercises in the *Introduction* neither reach the level of difficulty nor contain the variety of those found in Adam's two books. This, however, is understandable in view of the greater thoroughness prevailing among Continental tutors.

*   *   *   *   *

The preludes and fifty fingered lessons are arranged in a bilateral circle of fifths (C, a, F, d, G, e) as far as E major and c minor. The very short, almost improvisational preludes demonstrate the primary harmonic formulae in each key and provide a modicum of digital exercise. Aside from these, no pieces by Clementi are included. Here the author's commercial instincts are obvious—the tutor would sell on its own; his pieces would be bought separately. It is no accident, then, that the availability of his *Six Progressive fingered SONATINAS* (Op. 36) as a "SUPPLEMENT" to this volume is advertised on the title page.

This tutor represents one of the first major attempts to include music by well-known composers in the repertoire for lessons, rather than mere exercises or short, often dull pieces in binary form hastily written by the author.[40] The mixture of some first-rate keyboard pieces with

---

[40] On the title page of his *Art of Fingering* (London: W. Randall & I. Abell, [1770?]), Johann Caspar Heck advertised graded lessons by "some of the most Eminent masters," but there are only fifteen short unidentified pieces, probably by Heck, four by C.P.E. Bach, and one each by Benda, Kirnberger, and Handel.

A more interesting precedent is that of Adam's *Méthode du Doigté* of 1798, in which excerpts of major works are used to illustrate fingering.

popular airs, favorite songs and incidental music from operas and oratorios (the majority by Handel), and transcriptions of movements from instrumental music (most notably Corelli's violin and trio sonatas), was chosen with an eye on public taste and amusement as well as on the cultivation of good taste and the necessary development of technical skill. Critics praised the selection, which reflects the musical attitudes in England as well as the taste of its compiler.

Popular airs, including folk tunes, were a highly fashionable part of keyboard repertoire at this time, and Clementi recommended in a letter to Pleyel that he use Scottish or Russian songs in his sonatas "as an attraction for amateurs, whose palates are tickled by them."[41] Popularity of "the old masters" was also very strong in England, nurtured by the "Concert of Antient Music" that existed from 1776 to 1848 specifically for the performance of music that was more than twenty years old. Handel and Corelli were among the most frequently performed composers—a fact that Clementi did not overlook. Later on, many keyboard instruction books contained adaptations of pieces from operas, and throughout much of the nineteenth century piano arrangements of the current opera favorites were standard fare in the concert hall as well as the home.

The eleven transcriptions from Corelli's string music comprise twenty per cent of the lessons! Inclusion of this material can be attributed to Clementi's genuine fondness for the music of his fellow countryman,[42] to his stated belief in its usefulness for developing keyboard technique, and to Corelli's general favor in England. The *Allemanda* (page 30) and the *Allegro* (page 52), removed from the *Introduction* to the *Appendix* and later to the *Second Part of Clementi's Introduction*, are described in the list of contents of the latter as "an excellent exercise" for the left and right hands respectively. Eight of the eleven pieces by Corelli have sixteenth-note passage work for one hand or the other, and one has parallel thirds in the opposite hand. Lesson 45, an *Adagio*, obviously illustrates the legato style of chord playing, utilizing silent finger-changing where necessary.

Clementi's arrangement of two Mozart Minuets and Trios (Lessons 13 and 32) originally written for small ensembles of stringed and wind instruments is less readily explainable; Mozart had written some little keyboard pieces that were just as easy (or easier) and in some cases more attractive. Perhaps these pieces were favorites of Clementi's, or were particularly popular in England. In any case, Lesson 13 affords an example of what today would be considered untenable editorial practice. The "Minuet" is actually the *Trio* to the first *Minuet* of K. 599, while the *Trio* is the *Trio* to the second *Minuet* of K. 601! Both pieces were originally in C major. (Lesson 32 is the first *Minuet and Trio* of K. 604.)

Clementi transposed seven other lessons in addition to Lesson 13, presumably to distribute the pieces he wanted to use satisfactorily among the keys in an appropriate order. He transposed not only five lessons that he also transcribed for piano (1, 3, 8, 9, 13), but three keyboard pieces as well. Lesson 25 by Handel was originally in F major and was entitled "Courante." Lesson 46, "La Marche des Gris-vêtus" from the "4ᵉ Ordre" of *Pièces de Clavecin* by Couperin was also written in F major. Lesson 47, "Allegretto," properly titled "La Babet," from Couperin's "2ᵉ Ordre," was in D minor.

Of the lessons originally written for the keyboard, twelve had been composed much earlier for harpsichord or clavichord. Clementi's choice of these pieces by Handel, F. Couperin,

---

[41] Georges de St. Foix, "Haydn and Clementi," *The Musical Quarterly* XVIII/2 (April 1932), 258.

[42] Around 1800, Clementi published *A new edition of Corelli's Twelve Solos for the violin & violincello, with a thorough bass for the piano forte or harpsichord, in which a simple method is adopted for facilitating the reading of the tenor clef*, Op. 5 (Tyson, op. cit., 129). However, only three of the eleven pieces in the *Introduction* are from this set, six of the others being from Op. 4, and one each from Opera 1 and 2.

J.S. Bach, D. Scarlatti,[43] Rameau, C.P.E. Bach, and Paradies are well suited to "form the taste" of young pianists, as contemporary critics were wont to write. Clementi nodded also to his contemporaries, Haydn, Pleyel, Dussek, Cramer, and Beethoven.[44] As a group, however, the keyboard pieces he chose by these composers seem somewhat less interesting than those of the earlier musicians.

All attributions in the first edition have been checked, and forty-two of the forty-four are correct. The single known misattribution is Lesson 12, "Arietta by Mozart," which is actually an anonymous tune, *Freut euch des Lebens*, probably harmonized by Nägeli.[45] However, since at least one, and probably a second edition of that piece are known to have been published in London under Mozart's name prior to the *Introduction*, Clementi's error was certainly the result of the earlier misattribution.[46] Of all the rest of Clementi's attributions, only Lesson 34, by Cramer, cannot be confirmed from that composer's works available to this writer.

Of the six lessons for which no composer is given, 2, 18, and probably 19, are adaptations of folk songs. Lesson 20, "Fal lal la," is a Welsh song used in *The Cherokee*, a very popular opera "principally composed by Stephen Storace," according to the title page of the first edition, published in 1794.[47] Lesson 31, "Lindor," is the music by Antoine Laurent Baudron for the song *Je suis Lindor* in Beaumarchais' *Le Barbier de Séville*. Many composers, including Mozart and Clementi, wrote variations on it. This is one of the few lessons that Clementi used in all the editions of the *Introduction*, and he used this theme and five of his eleven variations, which had originally served as the third movement of the *Sonata in B-flat major*, Op. 12, No. 1 (published in 1784), in the *Appendix* and the *Second Part of the Introduction*.

The origin of Lesson 22, "Arietta," remains unknown. In the fifth and seventh editions of the *Introduction* it is marked "adapted by M.C." Since Clementi did not usually adapt short pieces originally written for the keyboard, this lesson probably stems from another source.

The lessons are arranged in order of key rather than difficulty. Clementi, however, was pedagogue enough to compile a list of the easier ones that should be studied first. To help the student, he also realized the trill and the beat in two of the very easiest lessons, 3 and 8, where they would be encountered initially.

Clementi's "editing" in the first edition consisted primarily of arranging the transcriptions and transpositions, and indicating the fingering. Generally, the transcriptions were done simply and accurately. Only in Lesson 1, which is an adaptation of "Das klinget so herrlich" from Act I of Mozart's *Die Zauberflöte*, did he alter the music beyond what was

[43] Scarlatti's harpsichord music was popular in England throughout the eighteenth century, partially as a result of the interest of his acquaintance, Thomas Roseingrave. In 1791, Clementi had published a volume entitled *SCARLATTI'S Chefs-d'oeuvre for the Harpsichord or Pianoforte*. The twelve sonatas in this collection (ten by Scarlatti, one by Soler, and one unidentified) are much more difficult than the four chosen for the *Introduction*. The latter are among the easier pieces (not the *Essercizi*) found in Roseingrave's edition of Scarlatti's harpsichord pieces published in London in 1739, and reprinted ca. 1754 and again ca. 1790. Sheveloff suggests that they are pieces dating back to Roseingrave's early meetings with Scarlatti in Italy. (Joel Lazar Sheveloff, "The Keyboard Music of Domenico Scarlatti: A Re-evaluation of the Present State of Knowledge in the Light of the Sources" [Ph.D. Dissertation: Brandeis University, 1970], I, 198; University Microfilms: 70-24, 658).

[44] Lesson 34, an *Andante with Variations* by Cramer, is the only piece in the first edition by any of Clementi's former students. With the exception of two Irish folksongs "adapted" by Cramer in the fifth edition, and *Scozzese* by Cramer in the eighth, the only other pieces by any of his pupils that Clementi printed in his pedagogical volumes are Field's *Polonaise in E-flat major*, in the *Appendix*, and a *Venetian Canzonet* by Mayer, in the eighth through tenth editions. (Presumably the latter is Charles Mayer.)

[45] Ludwig Ritter von Köchel, *Chronologisches-thematisches Verzeichnis sämtlicher Tonwerke W.A. Mozart's*, 6th ed. (Wiesbaden: Breitkopf & Härtel, 1964), 897.

[46] The earliest certain date of publication of this piece in England under Mozart's name is 1800, in the *German Museum* (London: C. Geisweiler). Mr. O.W. Neighbour has kindly informed the writer that among other editions of about this time attributed to Mozart is one by Bland and Weller with a 1799 watermark.

[47] Cecil Hopkinson, *A Bibliographical Thematic Catalogue of the Works of John Field* (London: Printed for the Author, 1961), 3.

necessary.[48] In addition to his rearrangement of Mozart's "Minuet and Trio" in Lesson 13 (described above), however, he presented the first two of Beethoven's *Sieben Ländlerische Tänze* as a single "Waltz" in da capo form (Lesson 39; they were printed as two separate lessons in the eleventh edition!), and omitted the *Trio* of Haydn's *Minuet* (Lesson 50) and the "Seconde Partie" of Couperin's *La Babet* (Lesson 47). Nevertheless, considering the prevailing freedom of performance practice in relation to suites, rondeaux, and other sets of pieces throughout the eighteenth century, Clementi's treatment of these lessons is not surprising.

Following the general practice of the times, Clementi added very few directions for performance to any of the pieces. Where there are additions to the composer's text (such as *Presto* for Beethoven's "Waltz"—certainly a misleading direction for a *ländler*—and *Andante* and *Allegretto* for Bach's *Polonaise* and *Minuet)* or differences in the ornaments from those in reliable sources (as in Rameau's *Tambourin*, and other pieces), it is impossible to ascertain whether Clementi used what he found in earlier editions or manuscript copies, or whether the alterations are his own. It is clear, however, that he made few such changes.

$$* \quad * \quad * \quad * \quad *$$

As a way of providing detailed bibliographic information for all known editions, and substantive differences for all of the English and some of the translated editions, a "List of Editions" is appended. Clementi's changes in the text of, and music for the fifth, seventh, eighth, eleventh, and twelfth editions as described in the "List of Editions," were attempts to keep the *Introduction* current. Changes in the text generally served either to make the material more explicit, or to bring it up-to-date, sometimes reflecting recent developments in performance style. Changes in the lessons were made with an eye to popular appeal and sales. The repertoire became easier, incorporating more national airs and sets of variations, often on well-known tunes. The public wanted newness in its tutors, and Clementi tried to satisfy the public.

In order to provide more sophisticated musical material as well as more advanced exercises for those who desired them, Clementi published an *Appendix to the Fifth Edition* of the *Introduction*. Along with extended "scale-exercises" in every key, which he composed, and many pieces based on popular tunes, the *Appendix* contains all the pieces by Corelli, Handel, Couperin, Rameau, Bach, Scarlatti and Mozart that were included in the four issues of the first edition of the *Introduction* but had been removed from the fifth edition in order to make the tutor easier and to give it a broader appeal. (These are listed on page xxxii).

In spite of its brevity, Clementi's *Introduction* is an important volume and the best of the English tutors of the late eighteenth and early nineteenth centuries. Although much was necessarily left to be explained by a teacher, the tutor provides considerable information regarding technical and stylistic details of performance on the pianoforte at this transitional period, and reflects many of its author's predilections. Its content is expressed so concisely that the significance of the remarks and examples runs the risk of being overlooked. A brief comparison with other methods published from about 1780 to 1820, however, makes that the significance of the remarks and examples can be easily overlooked. A brief comparison with other methods published from about 1780 to 1820, however, makes it all the more evident how much of significance is embodied in Clementi's work.

---

[48] The same adaptation of this melody, but with an accompaniment very close to that in the opera, appeared later as the first song in Volume III of *A Selection from the Vocal Compositions of Mozart, United to Original English Verses . . . the Accompaniments . . . arranged from the Original Scores by Muzio Clementi* (London: Clementi, Banger, Collard, Davis & Collard, ca. 1815), 6. In this volume Clementi identifies the source of the melody.

the "List of Editions." Alan Tyson was most generous in responding to queries, volunteering otherwise unavailable information, and making accessible his personal material. Frederick Freedman, Music Librarian and Professor of Music at Vassar College, provided keen criticism and invaluable suggestions while this work was in progress. Others whose kindnesses in providing information and checking details are deeply appreciated include Michael Anderson, Rita Benton, Georgia B. Bumgardner, Frank C. Campbell, Charles Cudworth, Pierre Galliard, Franz Grasberger, Diana Haskell, Richard H. Hunter, Peter A. Ward Jones, Georg Karstädt, A. Hyatt King, Alfred Kuhn, William Lichtenwanger, Mary Lou Little, Hedwig Mitringer, O. W. Neighbour, Thomas Watkins, and Emanuel Winternitz.

Sandra P. Rosenblum

Belmont, Massachusetts
January 1973

LIST OF EDITIONS OF
CLEMENTI'S
INTRODUCTION TO THE ART OF PLAYING ON THE PIANO FORTE
AND OF THE
APPENDIX TO THE FIFTH EDITION OF CLEMENTI'S
INTRODUCTION TO THE ART OF
PLAYING ON THE PIANO FORTE

I. Editions Published by Clementi

FIRST EDITION

Clementi's / Introduction to the Art of playing / on the / Piano Forte: / Containing the Elements of Music; / Preliminary notions on Fingering with Examples; / and / Fifty fingered Lessons, / In the major and minor keys mostly in use, by / Composers of the first rank, Ancient and Modern: / To which are prefixed short Preludes by the / Author. / Entd. at Sta. Hall. Price 10s,, 6d. / LONDON / Printed by Clementi, Banger, Hyde, Collard & Davis No. 26, Cheapside. / ☞ Where may be had, as a SUPPLEMENT to the above Work, / CLEMENTI'S Six Progressive fingered SONATINAS. / [right] R. Williamson, Sc.

Date: Entered at Stationers' Hall on October 26, 1801.

Collation: 63 pages, upright.

Location: (Arranged according to issue. See below for explanation.)

First issue: Houghton Library, Harvard University (title page lacking); Bodleian Library, Oxford University.

Second issue [from which this reprint was photographically reproduced]: Sibley Music Library, Eastman School of Music; S. P. Rosenblum (WM 1804). Title page and interior of Rosenblum copy heavily worn; "Williamson" no longer legible on title page, probably due to heavy use.

Third issue: Library of Congress; Newberry Library (title page lacking); Cornell University (WM 1806). Engraver's name appears to be lacking in this group, probably due to light inking, considerable wear of the plate, or both.

Fourth issue: Music Division, New York Public Library. Engraver's name lacking.

First editions not examined: Fitzwilliam Museum, University of Cambridge; British Museum; Pendlebury Library of Music, University of Cambridge (WM 1805).

While Clementi was travelling on the Continent from the fall of 1802 to 1810, his publishing firm continued to reissue the first edition of the *Introduction*. A comparison among the Rosenblum, Houghton Library, and New York Public Library copies reveals that while the *contents* of the three volumes are identical,[49] page 54 in the writer's volume had been reengraved and the NYPL copy had been completely reengraved, probably due to wear and cracking of plates. The reengraved plates were not proofread as carefully as the first set had been, for there are numerous omissions of slurs and dynamic signs in the lessons.

Further examination of copies of selected pages from the remaining first editions in American libraries, and of that in the Bodleian Library, led to a grouping of the first edition into four layers: the original issue; the second, in which only page 54 was made from a new

---

[49] The sole exception is the omission in the New York copy, for lack of space, of the note at the bottom of page 19.

plate;[50] the third, in which many pages were reengraved (including 10; 40 and 56, in which typographic errors from the first issue were corrected; and 54 again, with corrections of several errors that arose in the second engraving of that page); the fourth, printed from completely new plates.

The importance of this information lies in its relation to the "unlocated" editions of the *Introduction*. Of the eleven English editions published by Clementi, only editions identified on their title pages as second, third, fourth and ninth have failed to materialize in a fairly extensive search. The gradually reengraved second, third, and fourth issues of the first edition, with no special identification on the title pages, might have been considered press runs or reissues. But Clementi, back from eight years on the Continent, was eager to appeal to a new public, and must have deliberately chosen to consider them as "editions" when he elected to call the first *revised* edition the "fifth edition." "Second edition" would not have sounded as impressive.

SECOND, THIRD AND FOURTH EDITIONS—No volumes with these designations on the title page have been located. See explanation under the first edition.

FIFTH EDITION
CLEMENTI'S / Introduction to the Art of playing on the / Piano Forte, / Consisting of the / Elements of Music; / Preliminary notions on Fingering with / EXAMPLES; / Preludes & Forty fingered Lessons. / The Fifth Edition / Containing, besides other considerable Improvements, / VARIOUS NATIONAL AIRS / Adapted and fingered for the PianoForte / BY / the Editor. / Ent^d. at Sta. Hall. Price 10^s,, 6^d. / London, Printed by Clementi, Banger, Collard, Davis & Collard, 26, Cheapside; / where may be had Clementi's fingered Sonatinas, Op. 36; and an Appendix to the above Introduction, containing Preludes, Exercises, / National Airs, Variations and other pleasing and instructive pieces; the whole arranged and fingered by M. Clementi. / R & E Williamson, Sc. 8 Ban[d?] Str. West Sq.

Date: Announced in the *Morning Post* on February 18, 1811.[51] A search of the records of Stationers' Hall has shown that neither this, nor any other edition except the first and eleventh, were specifically entered there. Clementi must have assumed that printing "Ent^d. at Sta. Hall" on the title page of successive editions after the initial entry would provide sufficient protection from piracy.
Collation: 49 pages, upright.
Location: Music Library, Columbia University (WM 1810).

This is the first revision of the *Introduction*, published shortly after Clementi returned from his prolonged stay on the Continent. He was undoubtedly trying to appeal to a broader, less technically advanced and musically sophisticated audience, in order to increase sales

---

[50] The obvious difference in engraving, both in quality and design, between page 54 and its adjacent pages can be seen in this reissue. In the original issue the size of the staves, notes and "Clementi's Introd:" at the bottom of the page, as well as the styles of the F and G clefs and other details, match those on the surrounding pages. Further comparison discloses the following omissions and errors that were made in the first reengraving of this page:

> *Prelude* in B minor: slur omitted from four right-hand notes in bar 1; fingering for right-hand D in bar 1 should be 4; *rallentando* omitted from bar 4; sharp omitted before A in bar 6.

> *Giga: Allegro* at the opening of the piece omitted; tie from the left-hand B in bar 4 not completed; the left-hand note on beat 1 of bar 7 should be D sharp.

When this page was reengraved again for the third issue, three of the seven typographic errors were corrected (the missing sharp, the wrong note and the tie), but the time signature in the right hand of the *Giga* was changed to C.

The other differences in typographic design, such as the styles of the clefs or the sizes of the page numbers in this reissue, stem not from reengraving but from vagaries of circumstances when the first issue was produced.

[51] Alan Tyson, op. cit., 84.

of the volume. The majority of the lessons by Couperin, Rameau, Corelli, Scarlatti, Handel, Bach and Mozart which had appeared in the four issues of the first edition were removed (to be placed in the more advanced *Appendix to the Fifth Edition,* see page 00); and exactly half of the forty lessons in this edition are folk tunes, as compared to three of the fifty in the first edition. Most of these are Irish, Scottish and Welsh airs, which were extremely popular with all classes of the population at this time.

The preludes and lessons are in the easier keys, going only as far as B-flat major and D major, without the relative minors of the last two keys. For this edition Clementi wrote new preludes to replace those he was transferring to the *Appendix* (D minor, E minor, B-flat major, D major). The new ones are even more perfunctory than those in the first edition, indicating the haste with which the fifth edition was prepared.

Three lessons by Woelfl, Cramer, and Bomtempo call for more than the usual keyboard of five octaves, requiring the additional keys from f-sharp''' to c'''. Longer keyboards were gradually becoming more common, but Clementi did not include the added notes in the description of the keyboard until the seventh edition.

Changes of Text—Pagination and other indications for the placement of these changes and additions refer to the location according to the first edition. Unless noted, the changes remain in all following editions.

1. Page 2, par. 2, following "beginning by the FIVE lines": "then observing the LEDGER lines, and lastly the SPACES &c."
2. Page 3, added at the end: "This clef is used for the violin, flute, etc."
3. Page 4, added after the chart of note values: "Semidemisemiquavers, 64 to a semibreve, follow the same rule."
4. Page 9, end of first sentence, following "by which means, the strings VIBRATE SWEETLY into one another": "and imitate the BEST style of singing."
5. Page 9, added at the beginning of the list of terms: "Ped: signifies to put down the pedal, which raises the dampers; and this mark ⊕ means to let it go again."
6. Page 9, following "P, SOFT": "Più piano, SOFTER. Leggiermente, LIGHTLY."
7. Page 9, following "F, LOUD": "Più F, LOUDER."
8. Page 15: New scale fingering for F-sharp minor, right hand:

9. Page 16: New scale fingering for C-sharp minor, right hand:

10. Page 18, following sentence one: "N.B. The major part of the following exercises may be postponed at discretion, till the Pupil has attained some readiness of hand."
11. Page 20, replacing the list of easiest pieces: "There is but ONE WAY of PROPERLY fingering certain passages; but as a great number may be VARIOUSLY fingered, the author has preferred, throughout the work, that mode which he thought would produce the BEST EFFECT, and conduce most to the IMPROVEMENT of the HAND."
12. After the last lesson on page 49 is written: "To this volume is annexed an Appendix, containing Preludes, Exercises, National Airs, Variations, and other pleasing and instructive pieces: the whole arranged and fingered by M. Clementi."

SIXTH EDITION — A Spanish-language edition. Unlocated.
The advertisement for this volume in the *Morning Post* of September 25, 1811, reads as follows: "This day is published by Clementi & Co. No. 26, Cheapside. *INTRODUCCION a el ARTE de TOCAR el PIANO-FORTE,* by MUZIO CLEMENTI; translated into Spanish, and dedicated to the Spanish Nation. Sixth Edition in which is contained a variety of national airs of Spain and of other countries adapted for the Piano-Forte, by the Author." [Author's trans.]

By 1811 many editions of the *Introduction* had been printed in French and German by Continental publishers (see pages xxxiv–xxxix), and in 1809 a bilingual edition of the instructional material without the fifty lessons had been published in French and Spanish by André (see III, D, 9, page xxxvii). In a letter to his partner Collard, written from Vienna on April 22, 1807, Clementi mentions that he had intended "travelling towards Portugal and Spain," but the necessity of settling some family affairs related to the death of his brother had caused him to change his plans and head for Italy.[52] In spite of another, later, allusion to wanting to go to Spain, it remains unknown whether he ever reached that destination. Whether he wanted to arrange for a Spanish edition of the *Introduction* to be published in that country is questionable, particularly since there seems to have been little music publishing in Spain at that time. It was not uncommon for English publishers to produce books in other languages, and since Clementi was proud of his fluency in several European languages, he evidently decided to produce a complete Spanish edition himself.

SEVENTH EDITION
CLEMENTI'S / Introduction to the Art of playing on the / Piano Forte, / Consisting of the / Elements of Music; / Preliminary notions on Fingering, with / EXAMPLES; / Preludes and Fingered Lessons. / The seventh Edition / Containing, besides other considerable Improvements, / VARIOUS NATIONAL AIRS / Adapted and fingered for the PianoForte / BY / The Editor. / Ent^d. at Sta. Hall. Price 10^s,, 6^d. / London, Printed by Clementi, Banger, Collard, Davis & Collard, 26, Cheapside; / where may be had Clementi's fingered Sonatinas, Op. 36; and an Appendix to the above Introduction, containing Preludes, Exercises, / National Airs, Variations and other pleasing and instructive pieces; the whole arranged and fingered by M. Clementi. / R & E Williamson, Sc. 8 Ban[d?] Str. West Sq.

Date: Ca. 1812–14, based on the watermark of the copy located, and on the dates of the fifth and eighth editions.
Collation: 49 pages, upright.
Location: Bibliothek der Hansestadt Lübeck (WM 1812).[53]

The text of the seventh edition contains more changes than that of the fifth, many of which are concerned with directions for performance. The key scheme and preludes are the same as those of the fifth edition, and the repertoire of thirty-eight lessons is very close, the main difference being the inclusion of four new "Spanish" pieces—two boleros and two marches—presumably some that Clementi had arranged for the sixth edition, dedicated to the Spanish nation. Six lessons used in the fifth edition were omitted, including a *Scotch Air with Variations* by Christian Bach, an *Irish Air* adapted by J.B. Cramer, and one each of the few remaining pieces by Corelli and Handel (the *Gavotte* by Corelli, Lesson 36, first edition, and the *March in the Occasional Oratorio* by Handel, Lesson 38, first edition).

Changes of Text
1. Page 1: The "Scale, or Gamut", is extended in the treble clef to c‴, demonstrating a keyboard of five and a half, rather than five octaves.
2. Page 2: The "additional" keys are included in the description of the keyboard, in

[52] Max Unger, *Muzio Clementis Leben* (Langensalza: Hermann Beyer & Söhne, 1914) [reprint, New York: Da Capo Press, 1971], 163.
[53] Tyson, op. cit., 84.

the examples of treble notes on the lines and spaces, and also in the following exercises for treble and bass notes, which were partially rewritten.

3. Page 4: The semidemisemiquaver note and rest have been added at the end of the first brace.

4. Page 4, following the example of simple common time: "N.B. A composition marked thus ₵ was ANCIENTLY performed as fast again as when marked thus C; but now ₵ is performed somewhat faster than C."

5. Page 8: In the first paragraph on Style, after "means LESS STACCATO than the preceding mark;" there is the following rewording: "the finger, therefore is not lifted up so suddenly."

6. Page 9, following the conclusion of the initial sentence and the addition of the fifth edition: "SCIOLTO means FREE, neither Legato nor Staccato."

7. Page 9: Two marks are given to let the pedal up: ⊕ and ✳ [new]. (See changes of text in the fifth edition.)

8. Page 9, following "PP, VERY SOFT": "PPP, EXTREMELY SOFT."

9. Page 9, following "FF, VERY LOUD": "FFF, EXTREMELY LOUD."

10. Page 9: At the end of the comment on arpeggio is added "choosing the one best suited to the piece." The following additional choices are given:

11. Page 10: The material on the seventh staff is more explicit:

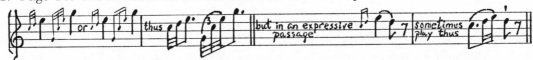

12. Page 11: The prepared shake on the seventh staff is slurred in one group of twelve.

13. Page 12: The final comment on the beat is more specific. "Lastly, let us remark, that the beat, especially the continued beat, is seldom used in modern music."

14. Page 14: "CON ESPRESSIONE, with expression. CON ANIMA, with great expression; . . ."

15. Page 14: "SOSTENUTO, in steady time, sustaining or holding on the notes their full length."

16. Page 15, top line: The sentence concerning unnecessary motion is printed in capital letters and set off with "N.B." [A "quiet hand" was central to Clementi's concept of technique.]

17. Page 15, top: The pupil is instructed to practise "the following passage, with the right and left hand separately; . . ." Following the simple exercise there is added "After a time, the passage may be practised with both hands together."

18. Page 15: Further instructions are also added for practising the scales. Following "daily": "but not with both hands together, till the pupil has acquired the greatest facility in playing them separately; extending each Scale 2 or 3 octaves more."

19. Page 16: The note on removing double sharps and flats is omitted.

20. Page 17: An example of the C major scale, aligned vertically for both hands and extending four octaves, is added.

EIGHTH EDITION

Eighth Edition / WITH / great improvements, / OF / CLEMENTI'S / Introduction / to the Art of playing on the / Piano Forte, / Consisting of the / ELEMENTS OF MUSIC; / Preliminary notions on Fingering, with / Examples and Exercises; / PRELUDES AND LESSONS, / Adapted and Fingered / BY / THE AUTHOR. / Ent. at Sta. Hall. Price 10^s. 6^d. / London. Printed by Clementi, Banger, Collard, Davis & Collard, 26, Cheapside; / where may be had Clementi's fingered Sonatinas, Op. 36; and an Appendix to the above INTRODUCTION / containing Preludes & Exercises, fingered by M. Clementi. / Hewitt Sc. 84 Charlotte S^t. Fitzroy Sq^e.

A sticker on the bottom of the page indicates that this copy was imported and sold by G. E. Blake, instrument maker, importer and publisher, located at 13 South 5th Street, Philadelphia.

Date: Between 1814 and 1816. Since the fifth, sixth, seventh, and eighth editions were produced in the relatively short time between February 1811 and circa 1814, it is likely that the Yale copy, with its watermark of 1814, may be from the first printing of the widely-used eighth edition. However, a watermark often antedates the actual publication date, as in the fifth edition, and other information must be used in trying to determine the upper limit of an initial date of publication for this volume.

Under the imprint of the publisher as given, the eighth edition would not have been published after 1818, when Banger dropped out of the firm. However, on evidence provided by the *Méthode Complette . . . par Muzio Clementi,* published by Carli in Paris, it is possible to suggest 1816 as the latest date for initial publication. Carli's address on the title page of the *Méthode* (see III, C, 3, page xxxiv) corresponds most closely to that given by Hopkinson for the years 1812–1816.[54] Since the first part of Carli's volume was based on the eighth London edition of the *Introduction,* the latter must have been available by 1816.

Collation: 46 pages, upright.

Location: Music Library, Yale University (WM 1814).

The eighth edition was rearranged, with the exercises and description of C clefs placed at the end of the volume, following the lessons. The section of exercises was expanded, with more stress on parallel thirds and sixths; the introduction of exercises for sliding the thumb and fifth finger from black to white keys; and with a greater number of exercises written out for the left hand, in some cases showing how to convert those that had been written for the right hand.

Clementi was also more thorough in following through the key scheme with the preludes and lessons in this edition than he had been in the fifth and seventh. He rearranged the bilateral circle of fifths, presenting sharp keys before those with flats, and he carried the sequence through to A major and E-flat major, and their relative minor keys. In the two previous editions the sequence had stopped at B-flat major and D major, without the keys of G minor and B minor.

Of the preludes, three are the same as those in the first edition, five are variants of those in the first edition, five are new, and the Prelude in B-flat major is an improved version of the one in the seventh edition. Three of the keys that have new preludes in the eighth edition also had new ones in the fifth. Apparently Clementi was not satisfied with those he had so hastily put into that edition, and decided to write better ones for the eighth.

The number of lessons was extended to fifty-three, with an almost complete change of repertoire. All but one of the Welsh, Scottish, and Irish airs that had figured so prominently in the fifth and seventh editions were omitted. Six new British folk songs were included and, in addition, eighteen songs of other nations: one German, one Tyrolean, two Spanish, four French, four Italian, five Russian, and one Persian, according to Clementi's attribution.[55]

---

[54] Cecil Hopkinson, *A Dictionary of Parisian Music Publishers, 1700–1950* (London: Printed for the Author, 1954) [reprint, New York: Da Capo Press, 1972], 21.

[55] At about this same time, Clementi also catered to the popularity of folk songs from the Continent with another publication, *A Selection from the Melodies of Different Nations . . . United to Original English Verses Never Before Published, with New Symphonies and Accompaniments for the Piano Forte by Muzio Clementi, The Poetry by David Thomson,* published in 1814. Surprisingly, only two of the melodies in this collection appear also in the eighth edition of the *Introduction.*

Handel, one of the previous favorites, is represented only with "See the Conquering Hero Comes" (Lesson 8, first edition). However, for the first time, Clementi included something of his own, the theme from the "Rondo" of the *Sonata in E-flat major*, Op. 12, No. 4. Pieces and arrangements of themes by Haydn (including the theme of the "Finale" of *Symphony No. 88*), Mozart, and Beethoven are present in greater numbers (fifteen) than in the first edition (eight), although the choices are much shorter and simpler than many in the first. This repertoire, with its very small proportion of pieces originally for keyboard, necessitated a considerable amount of "adapting," and Clementi was precise enough to indicate with double asterisks the ten pieces *not* so treated. These were either little keyboard pieces or airs already arranged by others, such as "Russian Air arranged by Dussek."[56]

Changes of Text

1. Page 1, after the title: "ADVERTISEMENT / This Book is not written with the visionary intention of superseding the indispensable aid of a master, but it is offered by the author as an assistant to the labours of both Master and Pupil."

2. Page 1: Description of the various clefs is as follows: "They are seven in number, but at present we shall only describe those two, which are NOW used in compositions for, the Piano-Forte. The other five shall be explained p. 46. The Treble clef, placed on the 2^d line   called also the G clef, as it determines the place of G   And the Bass clef, placed on the 4th line   called also the F clef, as it determines the place of F   "

3. Page 1, last sentence: "which places in the scale are distinguished thus ⌣ " is omitted.

4. Page 2: The exercise for treble and bass notes is now written in one brace, so that both hands can be played together conveniently after the notes have been learned. However, the "additional keys," f''' to c''', which were added to the exercise in the seventh edition, were removed in this and all following editions, perhaps to make it easier for beginning students.

5. Page 4: The description of the tie ends with the three tied quarter notes. The remainder is omitted.

6. Page 6: In N.B. following the chromatic scale, the reference to the "Harpsichord" is omitted.

7. Page 8: A second choice of realization is added for *tremando*, in which the lower C and the E are played together, alternating with the top C.

8. Page 9: The end of the definition of *Dolce* reads "SWELLING & DIMINISHING some notes."

9. Page 9, following the description of *OTTAVA* at the bottom: "When you see 8 under a bass-note play a lower octave with that note."

10. Page 9: The definition of "Ped." is at the bottom of the page in this edition, and the sign ⊕ for letting the pedal go has been omitted.

11. Page 10: The realization of appoggiaturas in the fourth line is prefaced by: "In the cantabile style, which means singing:"

12. Page 11: Preceding the third staff: "Shake, marked thus tr or ∿ or ⌄ or // ."

13. Page 11: The transient or passing shakes are realized as triplets.

14. Page 11: The English virginalists' sign for the beat, // , is omitted. After the five realizations, the description of this ornament is condensed to the following: "The LENGTH

---

[56] One obvious inaccuracy in this list is the double asterisk by Lesson 6, Handel's "See the Conquering Hero Comes." This chorus from *Judas Maccabeus*, originally in G major and ₵ meter, was adapted for the first edition (Lesson 8); Clementi then transposed it into C major, simplified the ornaments and filled in a few chords for the eighth edition.

of the BEAT is determined by the circumstances of the passage; and the under note
is mostly a semitone. In modern music, however, we make no use of the long or continued

Beat; but the short Beat ♪♪ has, sometimes, a good effect, for the sake of emphasis."

15. Page 14: At the end of the first paragraph, *MINUETTO A TEMPO DI BALLO* is
    omitted and *"NON TANTO,* not so much," added.

16. Page 15: To the suggestions for practicing scales with the hands separate at first,
    and for extending them for several octaves, both added in the seventh edition, the
    following is added here: "After learning 3 or 4 of the first Scales, the Pupil may play
    10 or 12 Lessons, and then come back to 3 or 4 more Scales, beginning with one
    flat, and so on in proportion."

17. Page 20 (18 in the eighth edition), immediately before the preludes and lessons:
    "The little Preludes are by M. Clementi, who has adapted all the Lessons excepting
    those marked with 2 stars."

18. At the end of the lessons, page 43 in the eighth edition: "The Pupil may now practice
    CLEMENTI'S fingered Sonatinas, Op. 36. New Ed^n with add^l keys."

NINTH EDITION. Unlocated.

Curiously, the missing ninth edition is followed by a tenth that is a reengraving of the
contents of the eighth. We can assume, therefore, that the ninth edition also had the same
content as the eighth. Since the numbering of new editions was by then well established,
and since Clementi was an astute businessman and promoter, it is more difficult to conjecture
about this missing edition than about the second, third, and fourth. Perhaps the ninth was
simply a small run and no copies found their way to a library. But it should be noted
that Clementi was on the Continent again from December 1816 to the fall of 1818. Since
the eighth edition was produced between 1814 and 1816, and the tenth probably around
1821 or 1822, the ninth might have been published sometime in 1817 or 1818, while Clementi
was away. It may have been a reprinting of the eighth, under the same edition number,
with the replacement of some worn plates; or the entire volume may have been reengraved.
These alternatives are analogous to those examined earlier in determining the relationships
among editions one through four.

TENTH EDITION

Tenth Edition / WITH / great improvements, / OF / CLEMENTI'S / Introduction / to the
Art of playing on the Piano Forte, / Consisting of the / ELEMENTS OF MUSIC; / Preliminary
notions on Fingering, with / Examples and Exercises; / PRELUDES AND LESSONS, / Adapted
and Fingered / BY / THE AUTHOR. / Op. 42. / Ent. at Sta. Hall. Price 10^s. 6^d. /
London. Printed for Clementi, Collard, Davis & Collard, N°. 26, Cheapside. / where may
be had Clementi's fingered Sonatinas, Op. 36; and an Appendix to the above INTRODUCTION,
/ containing Preludes & Exercises, fingered by M. Clementi. / Hewitt, sc. Carburton Str.

Date: Clementi's publishing firm operated under the name listed on this edition from 1818
    to 1822. This information, coupled with the watermark of 1821 on the copy in The New
    York Public Library, suggests 1821–1822 as the probable date of publication.
Collation: 46 pages, upright.
Location: Music Division, The New York Public Library (WM 1821).

The tenth edition is identical in content and pagination with the eighth, but was reengraved
in a different typeface. It is the first edition to bear an opus number.

ELEVENTH EDITION

Eleventh Edition / WITH / great improvements, / OF / CLEMENTI'S / Introduction / to the Art of playing on the / Piano Forte, / Consisting of the / ELEMENTS OF MUSIC; / Preliminary notions on Fingering, with / Examples and Exercises, Preludes and Lessons, / MUCH EASIER THAN IN THE PRECEDING EDITIONS, / Adapted and Fingered / BY / THE AUTHOR. / Op. 42. / Ent. at Sta. Hall. Price 10ˢ. 6ᵈ. / London, Printed for Clementi, Collard & Collard, 26 Cheapside. / where may be had Clementi's fingered Sonatinas, Op. 36; and an Appendix to the above INTRODUCTION, / containing Preludes & Exercises, fingered by M. Clementi. / Hewitt, sc Buckingham Place.

Date: Entered at Stationers' Hall on September 16, 1826.
Collation: 55 pages, upright.
Location: British Museum; Bodleian Library, Oxford University.

The text of the eleventh edition is very close to that of the tenth. Among its more interesting additions is "(According to Corelli)" after *Adagio* in the list of tempo indications, implying that Clementi had to justify his use of *Adagio* as the slowest tempo. It is quite possible that Clementi was challenged on the point, for most musicians at this time considered *Largo* or *Grave* the slowest tempo. For the first time, the scales are presented with the right and left hand notes aligned vertically, so that it is easy to read and play them together.

Of the fourteen preludes, nine are improvisatory variants of preludes in the eighth to tenth editions, three are the same as preludes in those editions, and two keys (G minor and E-flat major) have new preludes for the first time. The lessons are expanded to sixty, with the same key arrangement as in the eighth and tenth editions. A few pieces from the previous edition were eliminated, including four folk songs and the last remaining piece by Handel.

The new lessons in this edition show Clementi, as always, presenting what was *au courant* and popular: what he hoped would sell. They include, for the first time, opera arias by Rossini (three) and Weber (three, all from *Der Frieschütz*), composers whose works were then sweeping Europe, and four additional arias by Mozart (three from *Don Giovanni* and one from *Le Nozze de Figaro*). One of the arias by Rossini, "Di Tanti Palpiti," was said by Henry F. Chorley, the celebrated English music critic, to have been "the ruling London tune" around 1815—20.[57] Weber, of course, was an exceptionally well known figure in London during the 1820's; his operas were being performed frequently and he died there on June 5, 1826, just three months before publication of the eleventh edition. Another popularizing feature of this edition is the frequent explanation, in footnotes, of some of the directions for performance used in the lessons.

Changes of Text
  1. Page 1, following the "Advertisement" added in the eighth edition: "N.B. IN THIS EDITION MANY LESSONS ARE SUBSTITUTED FOR THOSE, WHICH WERE FOUND TOO DIFFICULT IN THE FORMER EDITIONS."
  2. Page 1, second line following the names of the letters, is added: "which are repeated as the scale below will show."
  3. Page 6, top: The note on Scarlatti's rhythmic notation concludes: "but this mode has not been adopted."
  4. Page 8: An introductory paragraph has been added to the section on style: "The style of the performance should be a true image of that of the composition. It is necessary, therefore, to study the character of the piece before we attempt to execute it. Here a good master becomes indispensable; for he must explain the peculiar nature of each composition, and furnish his pupil with the means of execution."
  5. Page 9: After the description of how to play chords with an added note, is appended: "This mode of playing a chord is called Acciaccatura."

---

[57] Henry F. Chorley, *Thirty Years' Musical Recollections* (London: Hurst and Blackett, 1862), II, 221.

6. Page 9: The sentence describing ARPEGGIO concludes: "which may be done in various ways, according to the style of the piece, or the fancy of the performer."

7. Page 11, third staff: The *tr* sign over the initial quarter note is used instead of the older \\ , and the second realization of the trill is:

8. Page 11, ninth staff: The first two realizations of the beat have a slight change in rhythm analogous to that of the trill noted above:

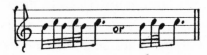

9. Page 13, explanation of terms of velocity: "(According to Corelli)" is added after *ADAGIO*.

10. Page 14: *CANTABILE* is defined as "in a singing, graceful and expressive manner."

11. Page 14: After the first sentence of PRELIMINARY DIRECTIONS is the following: "Let the elbows hang gracefully, rather above the level of the keys; neither too close to the body nor too far from it; and let the fingers and thumb be placed over the keys, always ready to strike; bending them in, more or less in proportion to their length, and accommodating them to the exigencies of the black and white keys. N.B. ALL UNNECESSARY MOTION MUST BE AVOIDED."

12. Page 15: The C major scale for both hands extending four octaves, which was added in the seventh edition, is eliminated here inasmuch as all the scales in this volume are aligned vertically in braces for both hands.

13. Page 18 (53 in the eleventh edition), at the head of the fingered exercises: "Exercises in fingering, which may be extended upwards, and downwards, at pleasure: to be used in proportion as the student advances."

14. Page 20, immediately before the preludes and lessons: "The little Preludes are by M. Clementi, who has adapted most of the lessons."

15. After the last page of the volume Clementi printed a copy of the title page of the *Appendix,* as an advertisement.

TWELFTH EDITION

Twelfth Edition. / WITH / Additional Improvements, / OF / CLEMENTI'S / Introduction / to the Art of Playing on the / Piano Forte, / Consisting of the / ELEMENTS OF MUSIC; / Preliminary notions on Fingering with a Set of New / Scales, Preludes, and Lessons; easier than former Editions, / TO WHICH IS ADDED, A NEW COLLECTION OF EXERCISES. / The whole Arranged, and Fingered, / BY / THE AUTHOR. / OP. 42. / Ent. Sta. Hall. Price 10/6 / London. Printed & Published by Clementi, Collard & Collard, 26 Cheapside. / where may be had Clementi's fingered Sonatinas. Op. 36, and an Appendix to the above INTRODUCTION. / Containing Preludes & Exercises fingered by M. Clementi. / Wm. Corette, sculp^t.

Date: 1830, based on the plate number 3388.
Collation: 57 pages, upright.
Location: Frank V. de Bellis Collection, San Francisco State College.

While the descriptive text of this edition is substantially the same as that of the eleventh, the remainder of the volume has several new features. Each scale is followed by the cadential progression $II^6_5 \ I^6_4 \ V_7 \ I$ in its key. Although the preludes and lessons are exactly the same as those of the eleventh edition (notwithstanding the alluring notice on the title page that they are "easier than former Editions"), a few more definitions, in footnotes, of the performance directions in the music were added to those that had appeared in the previous edition.

Finally, the section of fingered exercises was revised and enlarged. The first few exercises are much easier than those in the earlier editions, being concerned with simple stepwise patterns rather than repeated notes. Along with many of the older exercises (parallel thirds and sixths, legato octaves, silent finger changing and sliding from black to white keys), Clementi included in this section for the first time several passages, some with arpeggio figures, from his own works, Opp. 2, 25 and 27. New technical material consists of the exercise of holding some notes while repeating another, which was also used by Clementi in the early pieces of the *Gradus*. At the end, a considerable number of exercises are written out for the left hand alone.

Changes of Text
> 1. Page 13, explanation of terms of velocity: "(According to Corelli)" after *Adagio*, added in the eleventh edition, is deleted.
> 2. Page 14: "SOSTENUTO, in steady, moderate time; and sustaining the notes their full length."
> 3. Page 14: To the end of the last sentence on fingering is added "for which purpose see my Apendix to this work, my fingered Sonatinas, and my Gradus ad Parnassum."
> 4. Page 53 in the twelfth edition, introducing the revised section of fingered exercises: "A new Series of Exercises to be practised slow at first but with a firm touch; and to be used in proportion to the Pupil's improvement. N.B. Some of them should be postponed till the hand be full grown."

II. Editions of the Appendix

Appendix / To the Fifth Edition of / CLEMENTI'S / Introduction to the Art of playing / on the / Piano Forte, / Containing / Preludes, Exercises, National Airs and Variations, / with other pleasing and instructive pieces, calculated for the greatest improvement / OF THE STUDENT: / the whole arranged and fingered /BY /The Editor M. Clementi./LONDON, Price $\overset{\text{L s d}}{1.\,1.\,0.}$ / Printed by Clementi, Banger, Collard, Davis & Collard. 26 Cheapside.

Date: Entered at Stationers' Hall on April 6, 1811. Notice of entry does not appear on the title page.
Collation: 135 pages, upright.
Location: British Museum; Reid Music Library, University of Edinburgh; Library of Congress.

According to the British Museum, the *Appendix To the Fifth Edition* was reissued several years after the initial printing. They possess a copy of the reissue with a watermark of 1815. The Bodleian Library also has a copy of the *Appendix* which they date ca. 1815.

While travelling in Europe, or immediately upon his return to England, Clementi conceived the idea of making the *Introduction* a volume with broader popular appeal and of creating a volume of more difficult and somewhat more sophisticated works to supplement it. He quickly revised the repertoire of the fifth edition, as described above, keeping only seventeen of the easier pieces. The *Appendix* was published less than two months after the fifth edition.

The new volume follows the same systematic bilateral key scheme established in the first edition of the *Introduction*, but completes this scheme with "scale-exercises" through all the keys except the enharmonic ones. There are short preludes for every key through C-sharp minor. For D minor, E minor, and all the keys in the sequence from B-flat major to C-sharp

minor, Clementi used the preludes he had written for the first edition of the *Introduction*.
New ones or variations on the earlier ones were provided for subsequent editions of that
volume. The only keys for which new preludes were written for the *Appendix* are C, G
and F major, and A minor.

Each key through E-flat minor has a "Scale-Exercise," many of which are two pages
long and six of which are canonic throughout. These and the fourteen-page "Daily Practice,
or Circular Scale-Exercise thro' every key, major and minor," also written for the *Appendix*,
demonstrate the importance of scale work in Clementi's concept of technique. The preludes
and scale-exercises in this collection were subsequently extracted and published by several
European firms as *Preludes and Exercises in all major and minor keys* (see footnote 21).

All thirty-three lessons of the first edition that were not used in the fifth were included
in the *Appendix* (lessons 4–7, 9–17, 23–30, 34, 35, 41–50; most of those by Corelli, Handel,
Couperin, Rameau, J. S. Bach, Scarlatti, and Mozart), along with national airs, a few pieces
by other composers (including a *Polonaise* by Clementi's pupil Field), and several inconsequen-
tial ones by Clementi himself. He now had a two-volume pedagogical series.

REVISED VERSION OF THE APPENDIX

Second Part / OF / Clementi's Introduction / to the Art of playing on the / PIANO FORTE,
/ Being an improvement upon his Work formerly called / An Appendix; / Containing / Preludes,
Scale-Exercises, National Airs, Variations, / Two masterly Fugues of Sebastian Bach, / with
other pleasing and instructive Pieces calculated for the greatest / Improvement of the Student:
/ The Whole Arranged and fingered / by the Editor / Muzio Clementi. / (Memb. of the
Roy. Acad. of Music in Stockholm.) / Ent^d. at Stat^s. Hall. Op. 43. Price 1.1.0. / London,
/ Published by Clementi, Collard, Davis & Collard. / 26, CHEAPSIDE. / Hewitt, sc.
1, Buckingham Pl. Fitzroy Sq.

Date: Ca. 1821. Reviewed in the *Quarterly Musical Magazine and Review*, III/4[=No. 12] (1821).
Collation: Part First, 61 pages; Part Second, pages 62–125, upright.
Location: British Museum; Reid Music Library, University of Edinburgh (WM 1827); Royal
College of Music, London.

Unchanged reissue (according to Tyson) under the imprint of T. C. Bates; plate number
of "part the first": 1337.[58]
Date: After ca. 1833.[59]
Location: Royal College of Music, London.

Notice of registry at Stationers' Hall appeared again on the title page of the *Second Part*,
although it was not entered separately from the *Appendix*. Such notice appears to have been
used with some degree of freedom. (See note under date of the fifth edition.)

Although this writer has seen only title pages of the *Second Part of Clementi's Introduction*
(including that of Bates' reissue), by comparing the list of contents published in the review
in *QMMR* with the *Appendix*, it is possible to draw the following conclusions. The *Second
Part* is quite similar to the *Appendix* in purpose and type of content. There are the same
number of preludes and scale-exercises for each key, and they are probably largely the
same. Twenty-eight of the fifty-one pieces that had appeared in the *Appendix* were omitted
in the revision, including ten that were new in the *Appendix* (among them, five popular
airs) and eighteen that had come to the *Appendix* from the first edition of the *Introduction*
(pieces by Corelli, Handel, Couperin, Scarlatti, and Haydn). Among the thirteen new pieces
in the *Second Part* are two fugues by Sebastian Bach, the first of which, in C major, has
the heading "from an Original MS. of the author," a fugata by Handel, and several

---

[58] Tyson, op. cit., 86.

[59] Ibid., 86.

pieces whose authors were unknown to Clementi. Obviously, the revision was not intended to make the content of the *Second Part* any less difficult than that of the *Appendix,* but simply to vary it and to make a somewhat shorter volume.

The inclusion of the Bach fugues demonstrates once again Clementi's sensitivity to his musical environment, for at the turn of the century England was the scene of a considerable revival of interest in Bach's works. Between 1800 and 1801, two authorized English reprints of recent Continental editions of the *Well-Tempered Keyboard*[60] appeared.[61] Other works were published in London during the ensuing years, and between 1810 and 1813 a complete analytical edition of the *Well-Tempered Keyboard* was published by Samuel Wesley and Carl Friedrich Horn.[62] For his volume Clementi chose two Fugues from Volume II of the *Well-Tempered Keyboard:* the first in C major and the fourth in C-sharp minor. The source of the former was a manuscript in his possession, now in the British Museum, of Volume II of Bach's work, with which Clementi's text agrees in all the important details.[63] Most of the manuscript, including this Fugue, is in Bach's hand.[64] Since the Prelude and Fugue in C-sharp minor, along with two others, are now missing from the manuscript, it is not possible to ascertain Clementi's source for the second Fugue.

III. Editions of the *Introduction* Published in Countries other than England

For all following editions, ** indicates that the author has seen the volume, * that she has seen copies of the title page and other selected pages. For the remaining editions information was gathered through correspondence with librarians and from secondary sources. Listings marked "Whistling, 1828" were included in the second edition, published in 1828, of Whistling's *Handbuch der Musikalischen Literatur.*

A. Editions Published in the United States

1. ** Eighth Edition / WITH / great improvements, / OF / CLEMENTI'S / Introduction / to the Art of playing on the / Piano Forte, / Consisting of the / ELEMENTS OF MUSIC / Preliminary notions on Fingering with / Examples and Exercises; / PRELUDES AND LESSONS, / Adapted and Fingered / BY / THE AUTHOR. / NEW YORK / PUBLISHED BY J. A. & W. Geib 23 Maiden Lane

DATE: Ca. 1820–1821.[65]
Collation: 46 pages, upright.
Location: Music Division, The New York Public Library.

The *Introduction* was popular enough so that a New York publisher believed it would be profitable to reengrave and print the volume there, rather than to import copies, as Blake of Philadelphia was doing (see page xxvi). The engraver for Geib made a determined effort to have his title page look exactly like that of the London edition. Only a few minor differences in punctuation and engraving reveal that the page was printed from a new plate. The contents of the two editions are the same.

2. *Reissue under the imprint of GEIB & WALKER 23 Maiden Lane.

---

[60] This writer subscribes to Bodky's view of calling this work *The Well-Tempered Keyboard.*

[61] Hans F. Redlich, "The Bach Revival in England (1750–1850); A Neglected Aspect of J. S. Bach," *Hinrichsen's Musical Year Book* VII (1952), 293.

[62] Ibid, 290.

[63] Walter Emery, "The London Autograph of 'The Forty-Eight'," *Music and Letters,* XXXIV (1953), 108.

[64] *Ibid.,* 114 ff.

[65] Richard J. Wolfe, *Secular Music in America, 1801–1825,* 3 vols. (New York: The New York Public Library, 1964), I, 189.

Date: Wolfe dates this reissue between 1829 and 1843, based on the imprint.[66]

Location: American Antiquarian Society, Worcester, Massachusetts. (Two copies. One without a title page seems to be from a later impression since the plates are worn.)

B. Edition Published in Belgium

1. Clavierschule, kurgefasste, ein Handbuch f. Anfänger, Schott Frères, Brüssel, n.d.

Location: None. Listed in Pazdirek's *Manuel Universel de la Littérature Musicale* (1906–1911).

C. Editions Published in France

1. *MÉTHODE / Pour le / PianoForte / PAR / Muzio Clementi / Contenant, les Elémens de la Musique, et des Leçons / Preliminaires, sur le Doigté, accompagnées d'Exemples, / et suivies de Cinquante Leçons Doigtées, par les / Compositeurs les plus Célèbres, tels que, / Handl [sic], Correlli [sic], Rameau, Bach, Couperin, Scarlati [sic], Haydn, / Mozart, Clementi, Beethoven, Pleyel, Dussek, Cramer. &c . . . / PRIX 12^f Propriété Constatée de l'Editeur / A PARIS / chez Pleyel. [Plate number 457]

Pasted immediately below A PARIS, on the copy of the title page obtained by this writer from the Kungl. Musikaliska Akademiens Bibliotek, is a label of Chez JANET et COTELLE, M^{ds}. de Musique de Leurs Majestés Impériales et Royales.

Date: Several sources suggest 1801; Rita Benton has kindly informed this writer that the volume was registered for *dépôt legal* on March 14, 1802.

Collation: 63 pages, upright.

Location: Bibliothèque Nationale, Paris; Kungl. Musikaliska Akademiens Bibliotek, Stockholm.

2. Reissue with new title[?]: Introduction à l'art de toucher le Pianoforte, avec 50 Leçons.

Date: 1802 according to Paribeni and MGG.

Location: None. Whistling, 1828. Since there is no trace of an edition by Pleyel with this title, and since it is questionable that the firm would have published another edition in the same year with a new title it is possible that Whistling simply used a direct translation of the English title, (which was also used in that same year by Hoffmeister & Kühnel [III, D,4]) rather than the title given by Pleyel for the edition listed as C,1. Paribeni and MGG appear to have used Whistling's citation with no further verification.

3. * MÉTHODE / Complette / Pour le Piano-Forte / Par / MUZIO CLEMENTI. / Contenant les Principes de la Musique et des Leçons Elementaires / sur l'Art du Doigter, accompagnéa d'Exemples et suivis d'Exercices / graduels dans tous les Tons, extraits des Ouvrages des plus Célèbres / Compositeurs Anciens et Modernes. / Traduite et Rédigée en Français sur la huitième Edition de Londres. / Par Lélu, / Compositeur, Maître de Chant et de Piano. / Prix 30 fr, / Propriété de l'Editeur. Déposé à la Bibl^o. du Roi. / à Paris, / Chez CARLI, Editeur et M^d. de Musique, Place et Péristyle des Italiens. / (595)

Date: Ca. 1814–1816. This is the period during which the eighth London edition would have become available and Carli was at the address given.

Collation: 197 pages, upright.

Location: Newberry Library, Chicago.

The *Méthode Complette* is a combination of the eighth edition of the *Introduction* (pages 1–63), and the *Appendix to the Fifth Edition* (pages 64–197).

4. Reissue under the imprint of Vve Launer, the firm that acquired Carli's business in 1828.

---

[66] Ibid., I, 189.

Date: Between December 1839, when Launer's widow took over the firm, and 1854, when
E. Girod acquired the business.[67]

Location: Bibliothèque Nationale, Paris.

5. Méthode complète divisée en deux parties, Girod, Paris.

Location: None. Listed in Pazdirek's *Manuel Universel de la Littérature Musicale* (1906-1911).
Since E. Girod acquired Launer's firm in 1854, this publication may be a reissue, with
the new imprint, of the volume above.

6. Méthode de Pianoforte en 2 Parties, Carli, Paris. Whistling, 1828. The same sold separately.
Whistling, 1828.

Since no copy has been located, it is not possible to ascertain whether this is just the
Introduction printed in two parts, instructions and lessons (at one time Cappi printed just
the lessons [III,D,15] and André just the instructional text [III,D,7]), or whether it is
the *Méthode Complette,* with the *Introduction* as one part and the *Appendix* as the other.
Whistling is the only reference.

See also editions in French published in Germany, III,D,: 4,5,7,8,9,12,13,14,15,16.

D. Editions Published in Germany

Two series, one in German, the other in French, originated by Hoffmeister & Kühnel and
bearing plate number 104, are described as items 1 to 5.

Series In German:

1. *Clementi's / Einleitung in die Kunst / das / PIANO-FORTE/ zu spielen. / Enthaltend
/ Die Anfangsgründe der Musik; / Die nöthigen Begriffe zur Fingersetzung mit Beispielen
erläutert, / und / 50 LEKTIONEN / zur Uibung in der Fingersetzung aus den gewöhnlichsten
/ Dur-und Molltönen, nach den Mustern der vorzüglichsten älteren und neuern / Komponisten;
/ Nebst kurzen vorangehenden / PRAELUDIEN / vom / VERFASSER. / Aus dem Englischen
/ Wien, bei Hoffmeister & Comp. / Leipzig im Bureau de Musique / von Hoffmeister &
Kühnel. Preis 2 Rth. 16 ggr.

Date: 1802, based on the plate number 104, which appears only on pages 23–71, the plates
of which were used both for the German and French editions. The earlier pages have
no number. This volume is included in the advertisement of works published by Hoffmeister
& Kühnel in their German edition of Pleyel's *Méthode pour le Pianoforte,* dated December
1804.

Collation: 71 pages, upright.

Location: Gesellschaft der Musikfreunde, Vienna; Kungl. Musikaliska Akademiens
Bibliotek, Stockholm.

2. **A slightly altered variant with the following change in the title page after Aus dem
Englischen. Pr. 2 Rth. 8 Gr. / Neue verbesserte Auflage. / Leipzig, im Bureau de Musique
von A. Kühnel. Beneath this is a pasted label which reads: In Frankfurt am Mayn, bey
J. C. Gayl. / Weïssadler-Gasse Lit: F. No. 14.

Date: Between March 1806 and 1813, based on the publisher's imprint. Gerber, in his
Neues historisch-biographisches Lexikon der Tonkünstler, gives 1807.[68]

---

[67] Hopkinson, op. cit., 68.

[68] Ernst L. Gerber, *Neues historisch-biographisches Lexikon der Tonkünstler,* 4 vols. (Leipzig: A Kühnel, 1812-14), I, col. 744. Gerber
writes that Clementi's instructional text contains "nothing that cannot be found just as well in the instructions of [C.P.E.] Bach and
Türk," failing to observe the changes in technique, touch, ornaments or other factors of performance practice! He admires, however,
Clementi's choice of lessons in the first edition.

Collation: 71 pages, upright.
Location: Music Library, Columbia University (The Library of Congress' National Union Catalog curiously lists this copy under the imprint of C. F. Peters.)

A footnote added to page 2 of this variant reads as follows: "Note. The French designations in the plates of this work are there because they [the plates] are being used for the French edition." The French occurs only on a few pages where there is considerably more music than explanation. This scheme allowed the publisher to avoid reengraving the plates for the French edition. As in the first edition (D, 1), the plate number appears only on those pages whose plates were used for both the German and French editions.

The "improvement" in this edition seems to consist of a few sentences concerning invariable appoggiaturas on page 15, and some material on page 18 about major and minor keys. Typographic errors may also have been corrected.

3. Reissue under the imprint Leipzig, Bureau de Musique von C. F. Peters.
Date: After 1814, when C. F. Peters bought the firm from Kühnel's widow.
Location: Library of Congress; University of California at Berkeley. Whistling, 1828; Whistling and Hofmeister, 1844.

Series in French:
4. *INTRODUCTION / à l'Art de toucher le / PIANO-FORTE / PAR / Clementi. / Contenant / les premier Elémens de la Musique, / les notions nécessaires du doigter expliquées par des / exemples, et / L. LEÇONS / servant à l'exercice du doigter dans les tons majeurs et mineurs les plus usités, / d'après les meilleurs Compositeurs des différens tems; / précédés de courts / Préludes / composés / par / l'Auteur. / Traduit de l'Anglois / à Vienne chez Hoffmeister & Comp. / à Leipsic chez Hoffmeister & Kühnel. / (Bureau de Musique.) / Prix 2 Rthlr. 16 Ggr.

Date: 1802, based on plate number 104, which appears only on pages 23–71, the plates of which were used for both the German and French editions. Like its German counterpart, this volume is also included in the advertisement of works published by Hoffmeister & Kühnel in their German edition of Pleyel's *Méthode,* dated December 1804.
Collation: 71 pages, upright.
Location: Kungl. Musikaliska Akademiens Bibliotek, Stockholm.

5. *Reissue under the imprint: A Leipzig chez C. F. Peters / (Bureau de Musique).
Date: After 1814, when C. F. Peters bought Kühnel's firm from his widow.
Location: Bibliothek der Hansestadt, Lübeck; Kungl. Musikaliska Akademiens Bibliotek, Stockholm. Whistling, 1828; Whistling and Hofmeister, 1844.

A footnote on page 2 in this edition carries a message similar to that regarding French text in the German edition published by Kühnel: that the German designations on the plates of this French edition are there in order that the same plates can be used for the German edition. As in the first French Edition (III, D, 4), the plate number appears only on pages printed from the plates used both for the German and French editions. [It is possible that this volume was also reissued by Kühnel, as the German edition (III, D, 2) was, but no copy has been found.]

6. *English Edition:*
According to H. Baron of London, Peters published an English edition, using the same plates for the music, at about the same time as the French and German editions were published.

* * * * *

Editions published by André, two of which are bilingual and bear plate number 2738, are described as items 7 through 9.

7. Méthode pour le Piano-Forte par Muzio Clementi, André, Offenbach No. 2065.
Date: 1805, based on the plate number 2065.
Collation: 26 pages (the fifty lessons are not included), oblong.
Location: None. Information supplied by André Musikverlag.

8. *Méthode / pour le / Piano Forte / par Muzio Clementi. / 2de édition. / augmentée d'une traduction allemande. / Nr. 2738 Priz f. 2. / A Offenbach ˢ/M, chez J. André.

The Library of Congress copy has the following label pasted at the bottom of the title page, indicating sale of the volume in Russia where Clementi had a considerable clientele for his pianos: St. Petersbourg / Chez Charles Lissner, Magazin de Musique / Petite Morskoi, près de la place Isaac, Maison Manitscher No. 115.

Date: 1809, based on plate number 2738
Collation: 31 pages (the fifty lessons are not included), oblong. This volume is double-columned with the French on the left, German on the right.
Location: The Library of Congress; Bibliothèque Nationale, Paris. Whistling, 1828; Whistling and Hofmeister, 1844.

9. Metodo para el Forte-Piano por Muzio Clementi, Méthode pour le Piano Forte, par Muzio Clementi. Texte français et espagnol Nr. 2738. André, Offenbach
Date: 1809, based on the plate number 2738.
Collation: 31 pages (the fifty lessons are not included), oblong.
Location: None. Information supplied by André Musikverlag.

*   *   *   *   *

German and French translations published by Johann Cappi and his successors, some bearing plate number 1225, are described as items 10 through 16.

German Editions:
10. *Vollstaendigste / Klavier Schule / nebst / 50 Lectionen, mit vorangehenden kurzen Praeludien / zur Uibung in der Fingersetzung, aus den gewöhnlichsten / Dur, und Molltönen, nach den Mustern der vorzüglichsten / aeltern, und neuern klassischen Componisten, / von / MUZIO CLEMENTI / Ard Müll[er?]ᵈ / In Wien bey Johann Cappi / 1225

Date: Ca. 1806, based on the date known for the French edition (III, D, 12), the text of which was engraved somewhat later.
Collation: 65 pages, oblong.
Location: Bayerische Staatsbibliothek, Munich.

11. **Reissue under the imprint: In Wien bey Cappi und Comp: / Graben Nᵒ. 1122. (Plate number remains 1225.)[69]

---

[69] Whistling, 1828, has an entry for this publisher with the title *Einleitung in die Kunst das Pianoforte zu spielein mit 50 Lectionen u. Kurzen verangehenden Präludien*. Since no other source lists a Cappi und Comp. publication with this title, it is possible that Whistling was referring to this same edition but used the more direct German translation of the English title which had been used by other publishers (see III, D: 1, 2, 3). Whistling and Hofmeister, 1844, also lists the title *Einleitung in die Kunst . . .* under the imprint of Witzendorf, who became sole owner of Cappi's old firm in 1844 after it had passed through several other hands. This probably refers to a reissue of this edition.

Date: 1824–1826, based on the imprint of the firm.
Location: Music Division, The New York Public Library.

French Editions:
12. Introduction / à l'Art de toucher le / Piano-Forte / par / Muzio Clementi / Contenant les prémiers Eléments de la Musique / les notions nécessaires du doigter expliquées par des exemples, et / 50 Leçons / servant à l'èxercice du doigter dans les tons majeurs et mineurs les plus usités, / d'après les meilleurs Compositeurs des different tems, précédés de courts / Préludes / composés par / l'Auteur. / à Vienne chez Jean Cappi, Place St. Michel No. 4

Date: 1806, based on a notice in *Die Wiener Zeitung,* No. 96, November 29, 1806.[70] The plate number of pages 1–21 is 1284, indicating that they were engraved later than the German edition. From pages 22 to the end the plate number is again 1225, the same as in the German edition.
Collation: 65 pages, oblong.
Location: Gesellschaft der Musikfreunde, Vienna.

13. *Reissue under the imprint Vienne, chez Cappi et Comp.
Date: 1824-1826, based on the imprint of the firm.
Location: Österreichische Nationalbibliothek, Vienna

14. Reissue under the imprint of Witzendorf, who became sole owner of Cappi's firm in 1844. Whistling and Hofmeister, 1844.

15. 50 Leçons doigtées dans tous les Tons, tirées de la Mèthode, Vien, Cappi & Co.
Date: Probably between 1824–26, based on the name of the firm.
Location: None. Listed in Eitner.[71]

16. A volume titled *50 Leçons doigtées, par les compositeurs les plus célèbres* . . . (estratte dal Metodo) is cited by Paribeni as published by Cappi e Mollo, and also under the imprint Witzendorf. Eduard Mollo entered what had been Cappi's firm in 1839 (although Joseph Czerny had become the sole owner in 1828 and Matthias Trentsensky in 1832), and from 1844 on, A.O. Witzendorf was the sole owner. It is probable that Paribeni's references are to reissues of the volume listed above as 15. No copy has been found.

*   *   *   *   *

17. *CLEMENTI'S / vollständige / Klavier-Schule / Enthaltend / die Anfangsgründe der Musik / die nöthigen Begriffe zur Fingersetzung mit Biespielen erläutert / und / 50 Lektionen / zur Uibung in der Fingersetzung aus den gewöhnlichsten / Dur und Molltönen, nach den

---

[70] Alexander Weinman, *Verlagsverseichnis Giovanni Cappi bis A. O. Witzendorf* (Vienna: Universal, 1967), 62.

[71] Robert Eitner, *Biographisch-Bibliographisches Quellen-Lexikon,* 2. verb. Auflage (Graz: Akademische Druck- und Verlagsanstalt, 1959), II, 467. This work contains a list of seven editions of the *Introduction* in English, French, and German, and cites the libraries in which copies were located. These citations were checked, and several librarians responded that the volumes in question are missing. Only the following three copies remain at the locations reported by Eitner:
1. *Introduction to the Art of Playing on the Pianoforte,* Fitzwilliam Museum, University of Cambridge.
2. *Introduction à l'Art de toucher le Piano-Forte* (Vienne: Jean Cappi) Gesellschaft der Musikfreunde, Vienna.
3. *Vollstaendigste Klavier Schule nebst 50 Lectionen* (Wien: Johann Cappi) Hof- und Staatsbibliothek (now Bayerische Staatsbibliothek, Munich).

Muster der vorzüglichsten ältern / und neuern Komponisten; nebst kurzen vorangehenden / Praeludien / vom / Verfasser / 1407 / Wien bey T. Mollo.[72]

Date: Ca. 1806, based on the plate number 1407. Advertised in *Die Wiener Zeitung* of January 31, 1807.
Collation: 73 pages, oblong.
Location: Bayerische Staatsbibliothek, Munich.

It was this German edition that Beethoven procured through Haslinger for the use of Gerhard von Breuning.

*   *   *   *   *

E. Edition Published in Italy

**METODO COMPLETO / PEL / Piano-Forte / di / MUZIO CLEMENTI / Prima traduzione Italiana sulla quinta edizione di Parigi / N 647. FRANCISCO ALVARY. Sc=4:50. / Bologna / Litografia Cipriani e CC∿

Date: Ca. 1830.
Collation: 197 pages, upright.
Location: Music Division, The New York Public Library.

The *Metodo Completo,* like the French *Méthode Complette* from which it was translated, is a combination of the eighth edition of Clementi's *Introduction,* and of the *Appendix.* Pages 1–63 are the *Introduction,* with a few changes in the order of presentation of material, fuller discussions of a few subjects, such as the *fermata,* and definitions of some additional terms for performance (e.g., *mesto, amoroso, risoluto, religioso,* etc.). The list of terms of velocity in the *Metodo* begins *Grave, Adagio, Largo,* rather than *Adagio, Grave, Largo* as Clementi had always had them. (See pages xiii and xxix.) Which, if any, of these changes were incorporated during the production of the several French editions of the volume (the *Metodo* was based on the fifth French edition), and which during the preparation of the Italian edition, it is not possible to ascertain, since the writer has not seen any editions of the *Méthode Complette.*

Pages 64–197 contain the *Appendix.*

F. Editions in Spanish

1. Metodo para el Forte-Piano por Muzio Clementi, Méthode pour le Piano Forte, par Muzio Clementi. Texte français et espagnol Nr. 2738. André, Offenbach, 1809. (See III, D, 9, page xxxvii.)

2. Sixth Edition of the *Introduction* dedicated to the Spanish nation and published by Clementi, 1811. (See I, Sixth Edition, page xxiv.)

*   *   *   *   *

---

[72] Whistling, 1828, has an entry for this publisher with the title *Einleitung in die Kunst das Pianoforte zu spielen mit 50 Lectionen u. Kurzen vorangehenden Präludien.* Since no other source lists a publication with this title by T. Mollo, it is possible that Whistling was referring to this edition but simply used the direct German translation of the English title which had been used by other publishers (see III, D: 1. 2. 3).

INTRODUCTION TO
THE ART OF PLAYING
ON THE PIANO FORTE

Clementi's

Introduction to the Art of playing

on the

Piano Forte.

Containing, the Elements of Music;

Preliminary notions on Fingering with Examples;

and

Fifty fingered Lessons,

In the major and minor keys mostly in use, by

Composers of the first rank, Ancient and Modern:

To which are prefixed short Preludes by the

Author.

Ent.^d at Sta. Hall.

_Price 10.^s 6.^d

LONDON

Printed by Clementi, Banger, Hyde, Collard & Davis N.º 26. Cheapſide.

☞ Where may be had, as a SUPPLEMENT to the above Work?
CLEMENTI'S Six Progreſsive fingered SONATINAS.

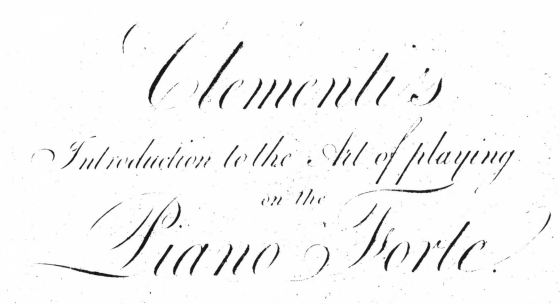

Clementi's Introduction to the Art of playing on the Piano Forte.

PRELIMINARIES.

All musical sounds are exprefsed by certain characters, called notes, which are named from the first seven letters of the alphabet: A, B, C, D, E, F, G.

A Stave contains five lines, and four spaces: the lowest line is called the first.

The notes are placed on the lines, or spaces; above, or under the stave; and the additional, called LEDGER lines are for the higher and lower notes.

CLEFS.

In order to determine the PITCH of musical notes, certain signs, called CLEFS or CLIFFS have been invented, which are set at the beginning of the staves.

There are five in general use.

The Bafs clef, on the 4th line   The Tenor clef on the 4th line

The Counter-tenor clef on the 3d line   The Soprano clef on the 1st line

And the Treble clef on the 2d line

The Treble and Bafs clefs are chiefly used for the Piano Forte.

The Scale, or Gamut;

shewing the position, and name of the notes.

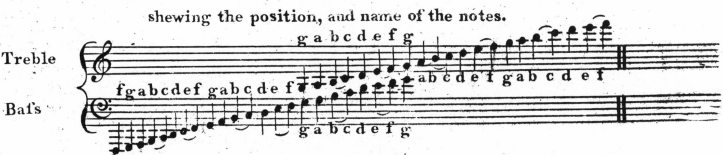

Treble

Bafs

Let the PUPIL now strike the notes on the instrument; taking notice, that the first LONG key, on the left hand, serves for the first F; the second LONG key for G; the third for A; and so on: making no other use, at present, of the SHORT keys, than as GUIDES to direct the eye; by observing, that between B and C, and between E and F, there are NO SHORT keys; which places in the scale are distinguished thus ‿

Remark on the foregoing Scale.

The first EIGHT NOTES in the treble-stave from G to G, are the SAME as the corresponding EIGHT NOTES, perpendicularly under them in the bafs-stave, both in NAME and SOUND; they are played, therefore, on the SAME keys.

As a help to memory; let the Pupil contemplate the notes, SEPARATELY, on the lines, and spaces; beginning by the FIVE lines.

Exercise for treble notes:

Exercise for bafs notes:

N.B. Let the Pupil FIRST be familiarized with the notes, by READILY naming them; and then find them out as READILY on the instrument.

Intervals.

An INTERVAL is the distance, or difference between two sounds in point of GRAVI-TY or ACUTENESS.

The least of our INTERVALS is called a semitone, or half-tone: it is the INTERVAL, in the NATURAL scale, between E and F; and between B and C. Ex:

The REGULAR progrefsion of the OTHER notes in the NATURAL, which is also called DIATONIC scale, is by an INTERVAL of two semitones or a whole tone.

Example of the NATURAL* or DIATONIC scale.

The INTERVAL between C and D, between D and E, or between any two CONTIGUOUS notes, in the scale, is called a SECOND: the INTERVAL between C and E, or between D and F, &c: is called a third; and so on.

NATURAL, from the FACILITY with which it is sung. and DIATONIC, as it proceeds chiefly by TONES.
Clementis Introd.

Example of INTERVALS

The INTERVAL of an 8th is commonly called an OCTAVE.

N.B. The nature, and name of the INTERVALS remain the same, whether the single notes be played SUCCESSIVELY, or whether two, or more, be struck TOGETHER: the form-er is properly called MELODY; and the latter, HARMONY.

Example of the latter. ——

The notes thus taken TOGETHER are also called CHORDS; the succefsion of which, played from certain figures set over a bass, according to a system of rules, is denominated THOROUGH-BASS.

Tenor, Counter-tenor, and Soprano clefs explained.

The notes written thus:

are played as if written thus:

when written thus:

are played thus:

when written thus:

are played thus:

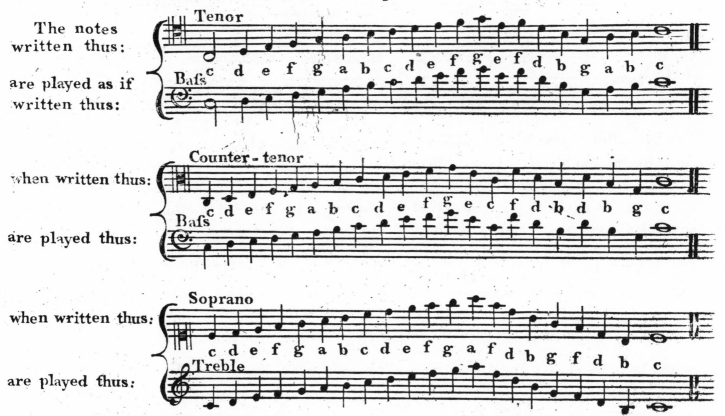

By which it is evident, that the Tenor-notes must be played one fifth HIGHER than the Bafs-notes: the Counter-tenor notes, one seventh HIGHER than the Bafs-notes: and the Soprano-notes, one third LOWER than the Treble-notes.

It is now proper to take notice, that the bafs-clef is also called the F-clef, as it indicates by its position where the note F lies: the tenor, counter-tenor, and soprano-clefs are called C-clefs, because they determine the place of C: and the treble-clef is called the G-clef, being placed on the line where G is found

Figure, Length, and relative Value of Notes; with their respective Rests.

Notes { Semibreve, minim, crotchet, quaver, semiquaver, demi-semi-quaver.

Rests {

One Semibreve ——— is equal in length of time to

2 Minims ——— which are equal to

4 Crotchets ——— which are equal to

8 Quavers ——— which are equal to

16 semi-quavers ——— which are equal to

32 demise-mi-quavers

A DOT after a note, or rest, makes the note or rest half as long again. Ex: is equal to a minim and a crotchet; or to three crotchets, and so on: is equal to and so on: by which it is evident, that the DOT to a minim is equal to a crotchet; and the DOT to a crotchet is equal to a quaver; &c: When a second dot is added to the first, the second dot is considered as the half of the first; therefore a double-dotted Crotchet, thus is equal to a crotchet, quaver, and semiquaver; or to seven semiquavers.

Let us farther illustrate this by the mark, called a TIE, made thus ⌒ which, when placed between two notes of the SAME pitch, binds the second to the first; so that only the first is struck, but the finger must be held down the full length of both. It is therefore indifferent whether we write thus or or and is the same in effect as

Time and its Divisions.

The BAR, made thus divides a musical composition into EQUAL por_tions of time.

TIME is divided into two sorts; COMMON and TRIPLE; each of which is either SIMPLE or COMPOUND: and the character or sign, which denotes it, is placed at the beginning of every composition, after the clef.

SIMPLE common time, when marked thus C or ₡ denotes, that each bar contains one semibreve, or its equivalent.

Example C or ₡

When marked thus 2/4 the bar contains one minim, or its equivalent.

Example

Four sorts of COMPOUND common time explained:

1st sort — containing 12 quavers in a bar, or their equivalent

2d sort — six quavers in a bar, or their equivalent.

3d sort — 12 crotchets in a bar, &c:

4th sort — 6 crotchets in a bar, &c

The two last sorts are very seldom used in modern music.

SIMPLE triple time explained.

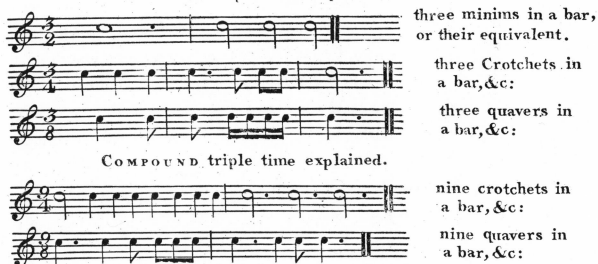

three minims in a bar, or their equivalent.

three Crotchets in a bar, &c:

three quavers in a bar, &c:

COMPOUND triple time explained.

nine crotchets in a bar, &c:

nine quavers in a bar, &c:

Compound triple time is seldom used in modern music.

N.B. The contents of every bar, in common time; whether SIMPLE, or COMPOUND, may be divided, (by beating or counting) into four, or into two equal parts: and in triple time; whether SIMPLE, or COMPOUND, into three equal parts.

The figures, which mark the time, have a reference to the SEMIBREVE; the LOWER number, showing into how many parts the SEMIBREVE is divided; and the UPPER number, how many of such parts are taken to fill up a bar. for example $\frac{2}{4}$ denotes, that the SEMIBREVE is divided into four parts, namely, four crotchets; and that two of them are taken for each bar: likewise $\frac{3}{8}$ indicates, that the SEMIBREVE is di_ _vided into eight parts, namely, eight quavers; and that three of them are adopted to compleat a bar. _____

The figure of 3 placed over three crotchets, quavers or semiquavers

thus  (which are called triplets) denotes, that the three crotchets must be per_ _formed within the time of two common crotchets, or of one minim; the three qua_ _vers within the time of two common quavers, or of one crotchet; and the three se_ _miquavers within the time of two common semiquavers, or of one quaver.

N.B. The easiest way is to consider them all as three to one, and to beat or count

Clementi's Introd:

the time accordingly; that is, to beat the first of every 3. (N.B. SCARLATTI, and others have written three demisemiquavers to a quaver; and three semiquavers to a crotchet in some of their pieces.) The figure of 6 over quavers or semiquavers, means that they are to be performed within the time of four of the same kind; which is a similar case to the preceding one. The figures 5, 7, 9, 10 &c: follow the same rule.

Sharps, and Flats, &c.

The SHARP ♯ placed before a note, raises it a semitone or half-tone.

Let us now observe a scale of semitones, called the CHROMATIC scale.

Ex:  The intervals of the contiguous notes are all semitones.

N.B. The LONG keys of the Piano-Forte, or Harpsichord, are commonly called the NATURAL keys, tho' they occasionally serve for SHARPS and FLATS; and the SHORT keys, are called SHARPS and FLATS, being only used for SHARP and FLAT notes.

Now if a SHARP be placed before C, thus: the note is called C SHARP; and it is found on the instrument between C NATURAL, and D NATURAL; being one of the SHORT keys: D SHARP is the SHORT key between D, and E; but between E, and F, there is no SHORT key; nor is it want_ed: for the INTERVAL between E and F, is but a semitone; and therefore when we want E, SHARP, we strike the key generally called F NATURAL. F SHARP will be found between F NATURAL, and G NATURAL: G SHARP between G and A NATU_RAL: A SHARP between A and B NATURAL: and B SHARP is under the same pre_dicament as E, SHARP; we therefore strike C NATURAL for it.

The FLAT ♭ placed before a note, lowers it a semitone or half-tone: and if the note is a B, to which the FLAT is prefixed, it is then called B FLAT; and it is found between B NATURAL, and A NATURAL, being one of the SHORT keys.

General rule: every FLAT is found by going one semitone LOWER; that is, toward the left-hand: and every SHARP, contrariwise, by going one semitone HIGHER; that is, toward the right-hand.

The double SHARP X raises the note TWO semitones; and therefore, if it be F double SHARP, we strike G NATURAL; &c:

The double FLAT ♭ or ♭♭ lowers the note TWO semitones; and therefore we go as much to the LEFT for a double FLAT, as we did to the RIGHT for a double SHARP.

The NATURAL ♮ takes away the effect of a SHARP, or a FLAT; whether single, or double. And ♮♯, or ♮♭, REINSTATES the single sharp, or flat.

The Pupil must by this time have observed, that is struck by the

SAME key as ♪ and ♪ by the SAME key as ♪ &c:

Now, the inconveniency of charging the memory with the VARIOUS uses of the SAME keys, is but small; when compared with the impracticableness of perform‑ing on an instrument, furnished with keys, PERFECTLY corresponding with eve‑ry flat, and sharp, single or double, which composition may require: a method therefore, has been adopted in tuning, called TEMPERAMENT, which, by a small deviation from the truth of every interval, EXCEPT THE OCTAVE, renders the instrument capable of satisfying the ear in EVERY key.

When a SHARP is placed close to the clef thus ♯ it affects every F throughout the piece; except where the sharp is contradicted by the natural.

N.B. The same rule holds, when there are two or more sharps at the clef; eve‑ry one affecting its corresponding note.

When a FLAT is placed by the clef ♭ it affects every B throughout the piece; except where the flat is contradicted by the natural.

N.B. The same rule holds, when there are two or more flats at the clef; every one affecting its corresponding note.

When a sharp, flat, or natural is prefixed to a note, in the course of a piece, it affects all the following notes of the SAME NAME, contained in the SAME BAR: it is then called an ACCIDENTAL sharp, flat, or natural.

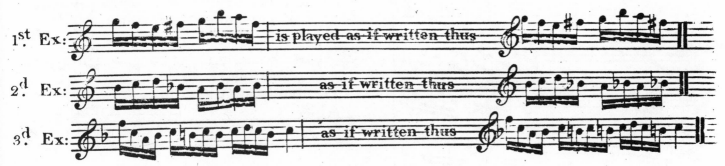

which abbreviations, are a modern improvement.

The foregoing RULE extends even to the first note of the subsequent bar, when the affected note is the last of one bar, and first of the next.

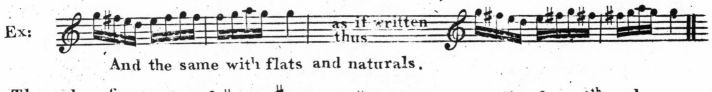

And the same with flats and naturals.

The order of SHARPS at the clef.  descending by a 4th and ascending by a 5th.

The order of FLATS at the clef. ascending by a 4th and descending by a 5th.

Clementi's Introd:

Various other marks.

The pause ▦ or ▦ renders the NOTE longer AT PLEASURE; and in certain cases, the composer expects some EMBELLISHMENTS from the perform_ _er; but the pause on a rest ⌢ only lengthens, AT PLEASURE, the SILENCE.

The SIGN or REPEAT 𝄋 is a reference to a paſsage, or strain, to which the performer is to return: the Italian words, AL SEGNO or DAL SEGNO, denote such a return.

The double bar ▦ marks the end of a strain; or the conclusion of a piece.

The DOTTED bars ▦ or ▦ denote the repeat of the foregoing, and following strain.   N.B. The second part of a piece, if VERY LONG, is seldom re_ _peated; notwithstanding the DOTS.

When the bars are marked thus ▦ or ▦ then the strain, only on the side of the DOTS is to be repeated.

Abbreviations.

The ITALIAN word, Segue; means, it continues, or follows:

Tremando, or trembling:

Style, Graces, and marks of Exprefsion, &c.

The best general rule, is to keep down the keys of the instrument, the FULL LENGTH of every note; for when the contrary is required, the notes are marked either thus: called in ITALIAN, STACCATO; denoting DISTINCTNESS, and SHORT_ _NESS of sound; which is produced by lifting the finger up, as soon as it has struck the key: or they are marked thus which, when composers are EXACT in their writing, means LESS staccato than the preceding mark; the finger, therefore, is kept down somewhat longer: or thus which means STILL LESS stac_ _cato: the nice degrees of MORE and LESS, however, depend on the CHARACTER, and PASSION of the piece; the STYLE of which must be WELL OBSERVED by the performer. The notes marked thus called LEGATO in Italian, must be played in a SMOOTH and CLOSE manner; which is done by keeping down the first key, 'till the next is struck; by which means, the strings VIBRATE SWEET_ _LY into one another.

N.B. When the composer leaves the LEGATO, and STACCATO to the performer's taste; the best rule is, to adhere chiefly to the LEGATO; reserving the STACCATO to give SPIRIT occasionally to certain pafsages, and to set off the HIGHER BEAU_ _TIES of the LEGATO.

This mark } prefixed to a chord signifies, that the notes must be played SUCCESSIVELY, from the lowest; with more or lefs velocity, as the senti _ _ ment may require; keeping each note DOWN 'till the time of the chord be filled up.

Chords marked thus are played as the preceding chords, with the addition of a note WHERE the oblique line is put, as if writ_ _ ten thus but the additional note is not to be kept down.

Dolce or dol: means SWEET, with TASTE; now and then SWELLING some notes.

Piano or Pia: or P, SOFT.

Mezzo, or mez: or mezzo piano, or poco P, or poc:P, RATHER SOFT.

Pianifsimo, or P^mo or PP, VERY SOFT.

Fortifsimo, or F^mo or FF, VERY LOUD.

Forte, or For: or F, LOUD.

Mezzo F, or mez:F, RATHER LOUD.

Forzando, or sforzando or fz or sf, to FORCE, or give emphasis to, ONE note.

Rinforzando, or rinf: to SWELL 2, 3, or 4 notes.

Crescendo, or cres: marked sometimes thus < means GRADUALLY LOUDER.

Decrescendo, or decres: GRADUALLY SOFTER; the same as the following; viz:

Diminuendo, or dim: thus > GRADUALLY SOFTER. N.B. this last mark > often denotes an EMPHASIS, where it is WIDEST, and then DIMI _ _ NISHING.

This mark <> means to SWELL and DIMINISH.

ARPEGGIO, or ARPEGGIATO, requires that the notes of a CHORD shall be played succefsively; which may be done in various ways.

Ex. Arp: thus or thus or thus or or

OCTAVA, All'8va, 8va alta, set over a pafsage, means that the notes are to be played an octave higher: and LOCO, that the notes are to be played again as they are written.

The APPOGGIATURA is a GRACE prefixed to a note, which is always played LEGATO, and with more or lefs EMPHASIS; being derived from the ITALIAN verb APPOGGIARE, to lean upon; and it is written in a SMALL note. Its LENGTH is borrowed from the following LARGE note; and in GENERAL, it is half of its duration; MORE OR LESS, however, according to the EXPRESSION of the pafsage.

APPOGGIATURAS, and other GRACES in small notes explained.

TURNS, SHAKES, and BEATS, explained.

N.B. The LOWEST note of EVERY sort of turn is MOSTLY a semitone:

The shake LEGATO with the preceding note, explained:

N.B. The GENERAL mark for the shake is this hr and composers trust CHIEFLY to the taste and judgment of the performer, whether it shall be long, short, transient, or turned.

The LENGTH of the BEAT is determined, like that of the other graces, by the circumstances of the passage.

N.B. When the note preceding the beat is an interval of a SECOND, let the beat adopt it, whether it be a semitone or a whole tone:

But when the beat, is on the FIRST note of a passage; or, when it follows a note, whose interval is GREATER than a SECOND, it should be made with a semitone; as the following examples will show.

Clementi's Introd.

Examples

Lastly, let us remark, that the beat is seldom used in modern music.

Major, and Minor Modes or Keys; VULGARLY called Sharp and Flat Keys.

The FUNDAMENTAL note, called the TONIC or KEY-NOTE, of a composition is either in the MAJOR, or MINOR mode. An exposition of the scale in each MODE, will best explain their efsential difference.

Ascending and descending scale in the key of C, MAJOR.

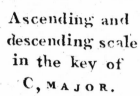

N.B. The intervals in THIS scale are in their SIMPLE state; but in the following, they are an octave higher, and are called COMPOUND intervals; still retaining their names of 2^d. 3^d. 4th &c: as in their SIMPLE state. The figure 1, stands for a note of the same pitch, called UNISON: this last remark is confined to the foregoing example.

Ascending and descending scale in the key of A, MINOR.

The first DIFFERENCE, which strikes the eye, is, that in the MAJOR-KEY, the semitone lies between the 3^d and 4th, and between the 7th and 8th both ascending, and descending: whereas in the MINOR-KEY, it lies between the 2^d and 3^d, and between the 7th and 8th ascending; but in descending, between the 2^d and 3^d and between the 5th and 6th. Authors vary, however, in regard to the 6th and 7th of the MINOR mode.

The ESSENTIAL and IMMUTABLE difference, therefore, between the MAJOR and MINOR key, is the interval of the 3^d, which differs by a SEMITONE; for if we analyse the 3^d in the MAJOR-scale, it will be found to contain two whole tones; or four semitones: Ex:

Whereas the 3^d in the MINOR-scale, will be found to contain one whole tone with a semitone; or three semitones.

Example

Now, the LAST, and if a chord, the LOWEST note of the bafs, in every REGULAR composition, is the KEY-NOTE; let the contents then of the first FULL bar be examined, (treble and bafs); where, if the 3.ᵈ be major, the piece is said to be in such a key major.

Example of a conclusion:  the LAST and LOWEST note of the bafs is F.

Example of the beginning of the same piece:  the 3.ᵈ of F, which is A in the first FULL bar, is MAJOR: therefore the piece is in F MAJOR.

Example of A MINOR ending. 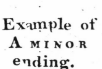  Example of the be- -ginning here the 3.ᵈ of A is MINOR, the piece is there- -fore in A MINOR.

N.B. Sometimes a composition in the MINOR mode may have a MAJOR ending; for which reason, it is safer to examine the beginning, in order to determine the MODE.

Let the Pupil remember, that the NATURAL major-key is C; and the NATURAL minor-key is A; which latter is called the RELATIVE MINOR to the former; and that every MAJOR-KEY has its RELATIVE MINOR in the same proportion, namely, one tone and semitone UNDER; as will be shown in the collection of scales.

Explanation of Various Terms.

The DEGREE of velocity in every composition is ascertained by some ITALIAN word or words prefixed to it: as ADAGIO, POCO ALLEGRO, &c. We shall annex a list of the terms mostly in use; beginning by the SLOWEST degree, which is ADAGIO; and gradually proceeding to the QUICKEST, which is PRESTISSIMO.

1 ADAGIO	6 ANDANTINO	11 MAESTOSO	16 SPIRITOSO
2 GRAVE	7 ANDANTE	12 CON COMMODO	17 CON BRIO
3 LARGO	8 ALLEGRETTO	13 ALLEGRO	18 CON FUOCO
4 LENTO	9 MODERATO	14 VIVACE	19 PRESTO
5 LARGHETTO	10 TEMPO GIUSTO	15 CON SPIRITO	20 PRESTISSIMO

Various other terms are sometimes added to the preceding, in order to modify or extend their meaning, as: NON TROPPO ALLEGRO, not too quick &c

We shall subjoin some of the most common, with their explanation.

MOLTO, DI MOLTO, or ASSAI, very. NON TROPPO, not too much. UN POCO, a little. QUASI, almost. PIÙ, more. MENO, lefs. PIÙ TOSTO, rather. SEMPRE, always. MA, but. CON, with. SENZA, without. MINUETTO A TEMPO DI BALLO, dancing - minuet time.

To determine more particularly the style of performing, some of the fol_lowing terms are also used: MESTO, or FLEBILE, in a melancholy style.

CANTABILE, in a singing and graceful manner. AFFETTUOSO, in an af_fecting and tender manner. GRAZIOSO, in a graceful and elegant manner. CON MOTO, with a certain degree of vivacity. BRILLANTE, with brilliancy and spirit. AGGITATO, agitated; with pafsion and fire. CON ESPRESSIONE, or CON ANIMA, with exprefsion; that is, with pafsionate feeling; where every note has its peculiar force and energy; and where even the severity of time may be re_laxed for extraordinary effects. SCHERZANDO, in a playful and light manner. SOSTENUTO, to sustain, or hold on, the notes their full length. TENUTO, or ab_breviated thus, TEN: to hold a note its full length. A TEMPO, in strict time. AD LIBITUM, at pleasure or discretion, with regard to time; introducing in certain cases an embellishment. TEMPO PRIMO, or PRIMO TEMPO, in the original time. RALLENTANDO or RITARDANDO, gradually slackening the time.

SMORZANDO, MORENDO or PERDENDOSI, extinguishing gradually the sound, 'till it be almost lost. CALANDO, or MANCANDO, diminishing by degrees the sound, or slackening almost imperceptibly the time; or both. DA CAPO, abbreviated thus: D.C., to return to, and end with, the first strain. VOLTI SUBITO or V.S. turn over quickly. The LATIN word BIS, means TWICE; it is generally placed over a pafsage within a curve line, which denotes the extent of the repeat.

FINGERING.

To produce the BEST EFFECT, by the EASIEST MEANS, is the great basis of the art of fingering. The EFFECT, being of the highest importance, is FIRST consulted; the WAY to accomplish it is then devised; and THAT MODE of fin_-gering is PREFERRED which gives the BEST EFFECT, tho' not always the ea_-siest to the performer. But the combinations of notes being almost infinite, the art of fingering will best be taught by examples.

PRELIMINARY DIRECTIONS.

The hand and arm should be held in an horizontal position; neither deprefs_-ing nor raising the wrist: the seat should therefore be adjusted accordingly. The fingers and thumb should be placed over the keys, always ready to strike; bending the fingers in, more or lefs in proportion to their length. All unnecefsary motion must be avoided.

Let the pupil now begin to practise, SLOWLY at first, the following pafsage; ob_ serving to keep down the first key 'till the second has been struck, and so on.

The + is for the thumb, and 1, 2, 3, 4, for the succeeding fingers.

Right Hand — and so on, a great many times.

Left Hand — N.B. Let every note be played even, in regard to time; and with equal strength.

Scales in all the MAJOR keys, with their relative MINORS; which ought to be practised daily.

N.B. The ♮♯ means that the double sharp is taken away, and that the note is to be played with a single sharp. The single flat is reinstated in a similar manner, after the double flat, as we have before remarked.

Clementi's Introd:

N.B. All the preceding Scales should be extended, in practising, 2 or 3 octaves more, as likewise the Scale of semi_ tones for the right hand:

and for the left hand.

N.B. The semitones are to be fingered in the same way, ascending and descending.

General Remarks on the foregoing Scales.

The right hand has the thumb on the KEY-NOTE or TONIC, and on the 4th of the KEY-NOTE, in the following MAJOR and MINOR keys: C, G, D, A, E, and B.

In all MAJOR keys with one or more flats, the thumb is put on C, and F.

The left hand has the thumb on the KEY-NOTE, and on the 5th of the KEY, in the following MAJOR and MINOR keys: F, C, G, D, A, and E.

In the MAJOR keys of Bb, Eb, Ab, and Db, the thumb is put on the 3d and 7th of the key.

Extensions and Contractions &c.

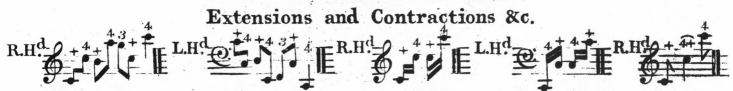

N.B. The 4+ means that after striking C with the 4th finger, the thumb is shifted on the key without striking it. In a similar manner the left hand thus:

Which mode of fingering should be much practised in various ways, the LEGATO-STYLE requiring it very frequently.

Clementi's Introd:

The shakes should be practised with every finger, not excluding the thumb; and upon the short as well as long keys.

Examples of fingering for the right hand.

But when the notes repeat too quick for the same finger, it is then necefsary to change.

&c: downward 9 or 10 bars longer, keeping down the thumb and every finger as long as pofsible; being one of the best ex ‗‗ercises for opening the hand.

But when wanted legato, thus:

When Staccato, thus: or thus:

Most of the pafsages fingered for the right hand, may, by the ingenuity and industry of the pupil, become models for the left.

Clementi's Introd:

To preserve the order of keys, some of the difficult are intermixed with the
easy Lessons: but the Pupil must practise the easiest first. Viz: N.º 1.2.3.7.8.9.12.15.17.18.19.
20.21.22.23.25.26.29.30.31 &c.

PRELUDE
in C. major

LESSON I.
Away with
melancholy:
by
MOZART.

Moderato

for: f (Heath edition)

LESSON II.
Aria.

LESSON III.
Air,
in ATALANTA;
by
HANDEL.

N.B. The shakes at the
end of the 1.ˢᵗ and 2.ᵈ part
thus

Clementi's Introd:

LESSON IV.
Air;
in SAUL;
by
HANDEL.

Moderato

N.B. The last bar of the 1st part is given twice on account of the difference of fingering in the bass.

Clementi's introd:

In the choice of fingering throughout the work, the author has consulted the best effect of the passage, and the greatest improvement of the hand.

LESSON V.
Dead March,
in SAUL;
by
HANDEL.

Grave

Clementi's Introd:

LESSON VI.
by
CORELLI.

Allegro

Adagio

Clementi's Introd:

24

25

LESSON X.
Sarabanda,
by
CORELLI

Clementi's Introd:

26

Allegro

LESSON XI.
Giga,
by
CORELLI.

Clementi's Introd:

LESSON XII
Arietta
by
MOZART.

LESSON XIII
Minuet and
Trio by
MOZART.

Clementis introd:

LESSON XIV.
Le Reveilmatin

by

COUPERIN.

Clementi's Introd:

N.B. The graces of the first
and second bar to be played thus

and so on
in a similar manner

PRELUDE in D Minor.

Larghetto

LESSON XV.

by
SCARLATTI.

Clementis Introd:

Allegro

LESSON XVI.

Allemanda,

by

CORELLI.

Clementi's Introd:

52

LESSON XIX

Triste Raison

Andante

LESSON XX

Fal, lal, la.
AIR in the
CHEROKEE.

LESSON XXI

Larghetto,
by PLEYEL.

The turn on the double note, in the 5th bar is to be played thus

LESSON XXII

ARIETTA
Allegro

ad libitum   a tempo

Clementi's Introd:

LESSON XXIII.
GERMAN HYMN,
with Variations
by PLEYEL.

Andante

dolce

Var: 1

sempre staccato

poco f

Var: 2

dolce

poco f

Var: 3

Clementi's Introd:

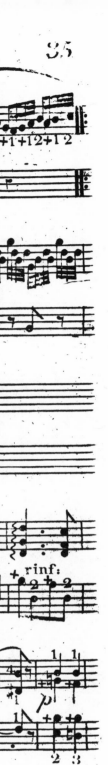

LESSON XXIV.

Andantino,
ma Moderato,
e
con espressione,
by DUSSEK.

Clementi's Introd:

36

LESSON XXV.

Allegro

by HANDEL.

LESSON XXVI.

MINUET in SAMSON

by HANDEL.

Clementis Introd:

37

LESSON XXVIII

RONDO
in the Gipsy stile,
by Dr. HAYDN.

Presto

Clementi's Introd:

Clementi's Introd:

PRELUDE in E Minor.

LESSON XXIX

TAMBOURIN by RAMEAU.

Vivace

PRELUDE
in B flat, Major.

LESSON XXX.

MINUETTO
by SCARLATTI

LESSON XXXI

LINDOR
an AIR.
Allegretto

LESSON XXXII

MINUET and TRIO
by MOZART.

A tempo di ballo

TRIO

Clementi's Introd:

Min: Da Capo

LESSON XXXIII

GAVOTTA in OTHO
by HANDEL.

LESSON XXXIV

Andante
with Variations
by CRAMER.

Var: 1

Var: 2

Clementi's Introd:

Var: 3

rinf:

Clementi's Introd:

PRELUDE
in G Minor.

LESSON XXXV.

Allegro

by SCARLATTI.

Clementi's Introd:

PRELUDIO
in D Major.

Allegro

LESSON XXXVI.

Allegro

GAVOTTA
by CORELLI.

N.B. The last note of the bass in the 1st part must be played with the thumb the 2d time, on account of the 1st note in the 2d part.

LESSON XXXVII.

MINUET in ARIADNE
by HANDEL.

dolce

LESSON XXXVIII

MARCH in the
OCCASIONAL ORATORIO
by HANDEL.

dolce

Da Capo al Segno

Clementi Introd:

LESSON XXXIX

WALTZ

by BEETHOVEN.

Presto

LESSON XXXX

Allegro

by CORELLI.

Da Capo

Fine

Clementi Introd:

LESSON XLII.

RONDO

by Ch: Ph: Em: BACH.

Andantino

Clementi Introd

Clementi's Introd:

58

PRELUDE
in C Minor.

LESSON XLIII.

MINUET
by SCARLATTI.

PRELUDE
in A Major.

LESSON XLIV.

Andante Allegretto
by PARADIES.

Clementi's Introd:

Clementi's Introd:

60

PRELUDE in F# Minor. **Moderato, e Legato**

LESSON XLV.

Adagio by CORELLI.

PRELUDE in Ab Major. **Moderato, e Legato**

LESSON XLVI.

SLOW MARCH by COUPERIN. **Un poco Andante**

Clementi's Introd:

PRELUDE
in F Minor.

Moderato e sempre legato

LESSON XLVII.

Allegretto
by COUPERIN.

Più tosto Vivace

Clementi's Introd:

62

PRELUDE
in E Major.

LESSON XLVIII.

POLONOISE and MINUET

by SEBASTIAN BACH.

MINUET.

LESSON XLIX.

GAVOTTA
by CORELLI.

PRELUDE
in C# Minor.

LESSON L.

MINUET
by Dr. HAYDN.

Clementi's Introd: